Secrets of

PILATES

Secrets of
PILATES

CATHY MEEUS
AND SALLY SEARLE

A Dorling Kindersley Book

Dorling  Kindersley

LONDON, NEW YORK, SYDNEY, DELHI, PARIS, MUNICH and JOHANNESBURG

This book was conceived, designed, and produced by
THE IVY PRESS LIMITED,
The Old Candlemakers,
Lewes, East Sussex BN7 2NZ

Art director *Peter Bridgewater*
Publisher *Sophie Collins*
Editorial director *Steve Luck*
Designers *Kevin Knight, Jane Lanaway*
Project editor *April McCroskie*
Picture researcher *Vanessa Fletcher*
Photography *Calvey Taylor-Haw*
Illustrations *Sarah Young, Catherine McIntyre,*
Coral Mula, Michael Courtney
Three-dimensional models *Mark Jamieson*

First published in Great Britain in 2001 by
DORLING KINDERSLEY LIMITED,
9 Henrietta Street, London WC2E 8PS

A CIP catalogue record for this book is
available from the British Library

Note from the publisher

Although every effort has been made to ensure that the information
presented in this book is correct, the authors and publisher cannot
be held responsible for any injuries which may arise.

ISBN 0 7513 3560 6
Originated and printed by
Hong Kong Graphics and Printing Limited, China

see our complete catalogue at

www.dk.com

CONTENTS

How to Use this Book   **6**

Introduction   8

The Pilates System   **10**

Preparing for Pilates   **34**

Re-educating Body and Mind   **46**

Foundation Exercises   **70**

Progression Exercises   **142**

Glossary   216
Further Reading   218
Useful Addresses   219
Index   220
Acknowledgements   224

Beneficial
People of all ages will benefit from a well-rounded Pilates exercise programme.

HOW TO USE THIS BOOK
This book comprises five sections. The first introduces Joseph Pilates, charts the history of the development of his exercise methods, and examines why they are suitable for people of all ages. Section two gives all the information you will need before embarking on an exercise programme. Section three prepares you for the practical bodywork by explaining the basics and outlining a suggested routine. Section four takes a look at foundation exercises, offering in-depth explanations and step-by-step guidelines. When you have mastered this section and are confident with the foundation exercises you will be ready for the final section, which takes a look at more advanced progression exercises.

Further information

While the information presented within the pages of this book is useful to anyone considering taking lessons in Pilates exercise, it is important to understand that it is not a substitute for instruction from a qualified Pilates teacher.

This book is for reference purposes only, and ideally the exercises within it should be carried out under the supervision of a trained professional. Please see page 219 for some useful addresses to help guide you.

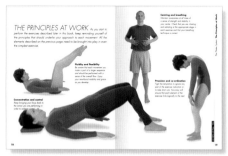

Background
The first section of the book looks at the basic principles of Pilates.

Planning
Easy-to-follow tables outline suggested exercise routines that you can follow on a daily basis.

Exercises
Each exercise is described in detail with step-by-step instructions to show you how to carry it out effectively.

Analysis
Black-and-white pages analyse each exercise and give tips on how to gain maximum benefits from your exercise programme.

Introduction

Mind and body in harmony
*The Pilates system of exercise
provides unrivalled integration
of mind and body.*

If you are seeking a balanced
approach to toning your body,
correcting alignment, and improving
your posture and co-ordination, then
Pilates is the perfect exercise system for
you to follow.

Mind and body

Modern fitness programmes
increasingly recognize the link
between the mind and body. Physical
practices to develop a healthy, fit body
also encourage emotional and
psychological well-being. Conversely,
effective mental relaxation and

meditational techniques help to dispel
the damaging physical consequences
of stress and depression.

The exercise system devised by
Joseph Pilates was one of the first to
acknowledge and build on this link
between mind and body. The aim of his
exercises is to use mental focus to gain
a deeper understanding of your body
and develop its potential for the benefit
of your overall health and well-being.
The emphasis is on developing your
mental awareness of how your body
moves – an insight that many of us have
lost – and is perhaps best described as
bringing your mind into your body,
rather than using your mind to gain
control over your body.

One of the differences between the
Pilates approach and that of many other
exercise systems is in the precision of
the individual movements that make up
each exercise. Newcomers to Pilates
often wonder how such tiny movements
can bring such enormous benefits. But
as you become more familiar with the
exercises, it will become apparent that

the system is so effective precisely because the movements are so carefully focused.

A personal journey

Embarking on a Pilates-style exercise programme can be seen as a first step on the path to a new physique and perhaps even a new approach to life. Pilates recognizes that every individual has their own capabilities and potential and encourages you to proceed at your own pace. Your developing confidence with each exercise will be your indicator of progress, rather than any arbitrary timescale or other external measure. This book aims to give the newcomer to Pilates an introduction to the principles of this exercise system.

Working with a Teacher

You can achieve a lot by practising the fundamentals on your own, but to progress you need the guidance of a qualified Pilates teacher. It is hoped that this "taster" will inspire you to join a class and make Pilates exercise a regular part of your life.

THE PILATES SYSTEM

Pilates is devised to bring your body back into healthy alignment and to teach new postural habits so that you can move freely without strain. The exercises strengthen the body from its "centre" to provide the stability from which harmonious and stress-free movement of the limbs can derive. ❧ It is important to note that the exercises need to be carried out precisely according to the instructions and therefore demand full mental engagement. ❧ This first chapter explains the background and principles underlying the Pilates system and provides useful anatomical information to help you understand how your body works and what happens to it when you exercise.

Joseph Pilates: The Man and His Work

Strong and supple
By following the exercise programme devised by Joseph Pilates you can achieve a strong, supple body.

Joseph Hubertus Pilates was born in Düsseldorf, Germany in 1880. As a child he suffered from asthma and rickets and this early experience of ill-health shaped his attitude towards the importance of physical fitness throughout his life. In his youth he made determined efforts to build and strengthen his body. He became an all-round athlete and also began to develop the system of exercises that he later termed "Contrology".

At the outbreak of World War I in 1914 he was in England teaching self-defence to British detectives. However, he was interned along with his fellow countrymen for the duration of the war and during this period he used his system of exercises to keep himself and the other internees fit and healthy.

After the war ended Pilates returned to his native Germany. During the early 1920s he began to work with some of the best-known dancers of the day. Then in 1926 he emigrated to the USA, where he founded his first exercise studio. By the 1940s his unique exercise regime had built up a growing reputation as a beneficial counterbalance to the sometimes damaging demands of dance training and he built up a wide clientele among New York's community of dancers and actors. There is no space here for a comprehensive list of the world-famous show business names who have benefited from the Pilates Method but celebrities such as Tracey Ullman are known to use Pilates. In recent years many sporting stars have also found Pilates exercises valuable for redressing the physical imbalances imposed by rigorous sports training.

The Pilates legacy

In the decades between the founding of the Pilates Studio and the death of Joseph Pilates in 1967, numerous students became proficient and knowledgeable in his methods. Some of these students went on to found their own Pilates-style exercise studios and there are now many different strands of Pilates teaching. Inevitably, each teacher gives their own emphasis and interpretation to the basic exercise programme that was laid down by its founder. Those who are interested in the authentic voice of Joseph Pilates himself can refer to his books, *Your Health* (1934) and *Return to Life Through Contrology* (1945).

PILATES PHYSIQUE

A Pilates-trained body is immediately recognizable for its symmetry and toned appearance. Key features of such a body include: a lengthened spine, in which the natural curves are neither flattened nor exaggerated; level shoulders that are free from any tendency to hunch towards the ears; the appearance of a long neck; a firm abdomen, without any bulging of the diaphragm; graceful, free-moving limbs; level hips; and strong, but not over-muscled, legs. Body movements flow smoothly and without effort from such a physique.

Key features

The distinguishing characteristics of a Pilates-trained body may start to become noticeable within a few months of starting regular Pilates practice. The progress you make will depend on your body type and the amount of time you are able to devote to your practice.

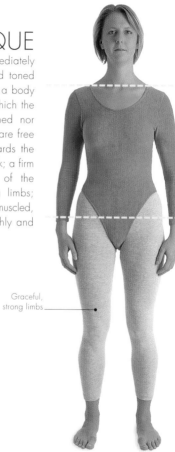

Graceful, strong limbs

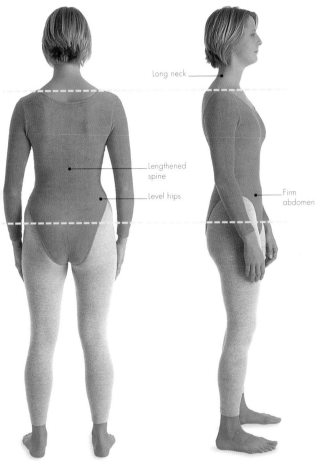

Long neck

Lengthened
spine

Level hips

Firm
abdomen

The Principles

Inspiration from the ancients
*Pilates based much of his
thinking on ancient ideas of
physical perfection.*

In devising his own system of exercises
Joseph Pilates drew on physical
training systems from many different
philosophical and cultural traditions.
He was particularly impressed by the
writings of the early Greeks, but was
also absorbed by various elements from
Eastern thinking and even studied the
movements of animals. The general
principles underlying each of his
exercises give testimony to the extent
to which his method is intended to
reach both body and mind.

Concentration and control

In Pilates the key to success is the
engagement of the mind in the actions
of the muscles of the body. This mental
focus encourages the development of
body awareness – this is a sensitivity
to the effect of different movements
and muscle actions on the body as
a whole. To achieve it you first need
to develop your ability to focus without
distraction on the movements you are
trying to perform in order to rediscover
"forgotten" muscles and ways of
moving. Only when you are
concentrating in this way will you be
able to gain control over your muscles
and move in the way you want to,
rather than being dictated to by habit.

Precision and co-ordination

Your aim is to perform each exercise
in precisely the way described. The
difference between moving correctly
and incorrectly is often apparently
minuscule to the newcomer to Pilates,
but gaining awareness of these subtle
nuances of body use is one of the key

lessons you will be learning. Ultimately the aim is to be able to link series of movements in a co-ordinated and balanced fashion.

Fluidity and flexibility

Pilates exercises are designed to encourage smooth movements that flow from one position to the next. There should be no hurried or jerky actions as these risk straining and shortening the muscles. The increased flexibility created by regular Pilates practice enhances the movement possibilities that are available to you and the fluidity with which you can perform them.

Centring and breathing

The Pilates approach aims to help you develop strength at the centre of your body, in the muscles of the torso, in order to free the movement of the limbs. To achieve this you also need to learn to breathe in a way that brings adequate oxygen into your body but that does not encourage excessive relaxation at the centre during exercise.

THE PRINCIPLES AT WORK

As you start to perform the exercises described later in this book, keep reminding yourself of the principles that should underlie your approach to each movement. All the elements described on the previous page need to be brought into play in even the simplest exercise.

Fluidity and flexibility

Be aware that each movement you make is part of a larger sequence and should be performed with a sense of the overall flow. Enjoy your new-found mobility and grace as you develop.

Concentration and control

Keep bringing your focus back to the action you are performing in order to achieve control.

Centring and breathing

Maintain awareness at all times of a sense of strength and stability in your centre. Check that you are inhaling and exhaling at the appropriate stage in each exercise and that your breathing technique is correct.

Precision and co-ordination

Fight the temptation to ignore any part of the exercise instruction or to take short cuts. Accuracy will ensure that each element of the exercise links logically to the next.

The Key Body Structures

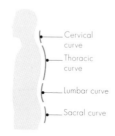

- Cervical curve
- Thoracic curve
- Lumbar curve
- Sacral curve

Natural curves

The four curves of the back provide natural shock-absorbing capability.

Before embarking on a Pilates programme, it is important to learn some basic facts about the key anatomical features that are of particular relevance to the exercises you will be performing. These features will also be mentioned from time to time during the course of the book.

The spine

The spine is the bony column that protects the spinal cord and also connects and supports the entire skeleton. The spine is made up of 34 separate bones known as vertebrae. This segmented structure gives the spine its flexibility and strength. Each vertebra is joined to its neighbour by ligaments that control its range of movement. Intervertebral discs provide a cushioning layer of cartilage that prevents friction between the vertebrae.

Viewed from behind, the spine should appear straight, but in profile it has four natural curves. These curves lend the spine a degree of springiness that allows it to absorb shocks that will be incurred during normal movement. One of the objectives of Pilates exercise is to maintain or re-establish this healthy profile, which can sometimes be distorted through poor postural habits.

The shoulders

The shoulders are the points at which the arms are joined to the torso. Each shoulder is a meeting point for three bones: the collar bone (clavicle), shoulder blade (scapula), and upper arm bone (humerus). The collar bone is joined to the top of the breast bone (sternum). The relative position of the shoulders is a vital determinant of the body's overall posture.

The pelvis

The pelvis is the bony basin that contains the body's lower abdominal organs. It is joined to the lower part of the spine and provides the attachment points for the legs – the hip joints. The vertical muscles of the abdomen (see page 22) are attached to the lower part of the pelvis – the pubic bone. Proper alignment of the pelvis is a key factor in maintaining the stability of the torso and is a priority in all Pilates exercises.

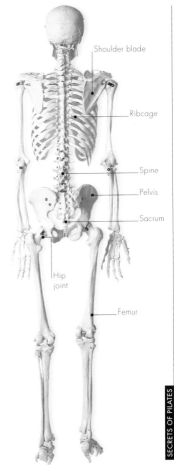

Shoulder blade

Ribcage

Spine

Pelvis

Sacrum

Hip joint

Femur

Strengthening
Many medical experts believe that Pilates increases bone density throughout the body, reducing the risk of fractures and disorders, including osteoporosis.

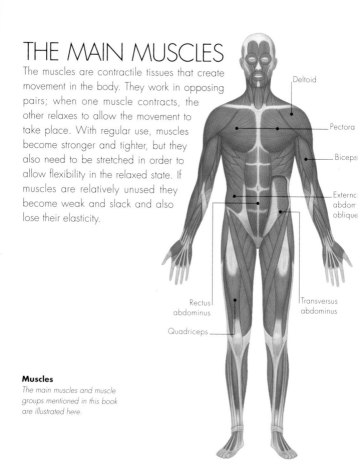

THE MAIN MUSCLES

The muscles are contractile tissues that create movement in the body. They work in opposing pairs; when one muscle contracts, the other relaxes to allow the movement to take place. With regular use, muscles become stronger and tighter, but they also need to be stretched in order to allow flexibility in the relaxed state. If muscles are relatively unused they become weak and slack and also lose their elasticity.

Deltoid

Pectoral

Biceps

External abdominal oblique

Rectus abdominus

Transversus abdominus

Quadriceps

Muscles

The main muscles and muscle groups mentioned in this book are illustrated here.

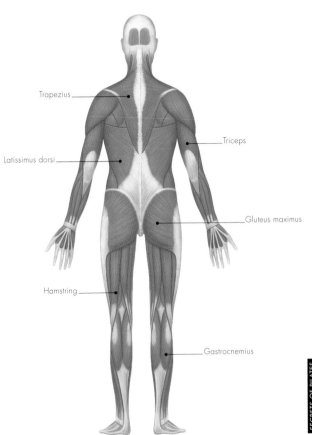

Trapezius

Triceps

Latissimus dorsi

Gluteus maximus

Hamstring

Gastrocnemius

The Girdle of Strength

A strong centre

All Pilates exercise relies on the stability provided by strength in the central girdle.

Acccoding to Pilates theory, all movement of the body should originate from a strong centre. Joseph Pilates called this the "girdle of strength" or "powerhouse". When the torso is held in correct and stable alignment, the limbs are free to move without strain. A strong torso, in which the muscles of the abdomen and back actively support the spine and internal organs, has a graceful, energetic appearance and is less likely to suffer from strains and injuries due to poor posture. If the girdle of strength is weak, the strain of moving or maintaining position is taken on by other muscles, such as those of the legs, shoulders, and back, which are not designed for such work.

The centring muscles

One of your first tasks as a Pilates beginner is to locate and become familiar with your girdle of strength. The body has its centre of gravity within the abdominal cavity just below the navel and this area should also be the stable centre of the torso.

Except when you are specifically aiming to reach a relaxed state, whenever you perform a Pilates exercise you will be instructed to engage your centring muscles. This means you should tighten, without tensing, your abdominal muscles on the out-breath. When you do this you should visualize your navel being drawn towards your spine ("navel to spine" is a common mantra). You also need to engage your pelvic floor (see pages 54–55), buttock muscles, and the latissimus dorsi (lats).

Maintaining muscle tone

Some forms of exercise increase muscle bulk as well as physical strength, but the effect of Pilates is to tone and lengthen the muscles, creating the possibility of a wide range of movements in a well-balanced body.

Getting into good habits

Regularly reminding yourself to engage your centring muscles before undertaking any kind of movement, particularly a potentially strenuous lifting task, is a valuable way of building the principles of Pilates into your everyday life. If you do nothing else in terms of regular Pilates practice, this action alone will bring benefits as it will protect you from injury while you are undertaking normal tasks. Good habits as well as bad ones can become second nature and you will soon find that you will be engaging your centring muscles without conscious effort. You will find that as you practise engaging your "girdle of strength" your body will benefit from increased stability.

STRONG CENTRE IN ACTION

When you engage your centring muscles you are freeing your body to move in a safe and harmonious way. As your abdominal muscles become stronger with regular Pilates practice, you will find that you can move with increasing fluidity and ease. The illustrations here show how engaging the centring muscles will ease movement in a variety of positions.

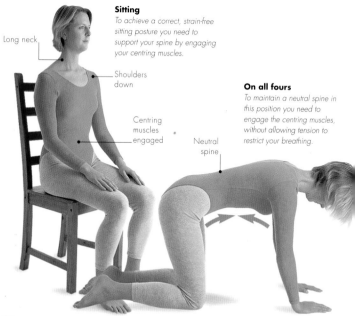

Sitting

To achieve a correct, strain-free sitting posture you need to support your spine by engaging your centring muscles.

Long neck

Shoulders down

Centring muscles engaged

On all fours

To maintain a neutral spine in this position you need to engage the centring muscles, without allowing tension to restrict your breathing.

Neutral spine

Standing at ease

This apparently relaxed posture is achieved only when the muscles of the abdomen are fully engaged supporting the spine and preventing loss of alignment.

Flexing forward

In this position the spine is extremely vulnerable unless it is supported by strongly engaged centring muscles. This is especially important if you are lifting a weight from this position.

Spine supported by centring muscles

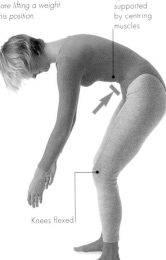

Knees flexed

Who Benefits from Pilates?

Sport and Pilates
Pilates exercise is a perfect adjunct to serious sports training.

Pilates has an unrivalled track record as a safe and effective method of body conditioning for people of all ages. It can also help to redress physical imbalances that have arisen from ingrained, poor postural habits.

Back pain

Many people try Pilates because they are suffering from back pain caused by postural faults. The emphasis that Pilates places on strengthening the support that the abdominal muscles give to the spine is just what back pain sufferers need.

Occupational problems

Many forms of sports or dance training focus on particular actions that are relevant to that activity, and this often leads to bodily imbalances. For example, a tennis player will use and develop muscles on the side on which he or she holds the racquet. This can force the body out of alignment and strain and injury are a common consequence. Those engaged in occupations that involve repetitive movements, such as computer operators or assembly-line workers, are similarly at risk from strain. Pilates helps to prevent and correct such imbalances, and supports recovery from injury.

Joint problems

Strain on the joints is often the result of failure to engage the appropriate muscles involved in a particular action of the body. This can exacerbate chronic inflammation of the joints (arthritis) and in some cases may be a contributory cause. Pilates teaches you to use your body in way that is free

from excessive strain and it strengthens
key muscles that protect weight-bearing
joints such as the hips and knees.

Body beautiful

Perhaps the majority of Pilates students
are inspired by the prospect of
developing a more streamlined figure.
One of the key benefits of this form of
exercise is that it tones the muscles and
helps you achieve a flatter stomach,
tighter buttocks, and firmer thighs.
However, Pilates is not primarily a fat-
burning form of exercise. If you are
carrying excess body fat, your
appearance will still benefit from Pilates
training, but if you are anxious to lose
weight, you may need to make dietary
adjustments and add some aerobic
activity, such as regular walking, to
your Pilates practice.

A Word of Warning

Be sure to read the advice on getting started
on page 36 before embarking on any of the
exercises in this book.

Sportspeople
You can help to minimize sports injuries by adding Pilates exercise to your regular training.

PILATES FOR EVERYONE
Pilates exercise is suitable for people of all ages. It has as much relevance for older people entering retirement as it does for those in the prime of life. Provided that proper caution is observed and expert advice sought when appropriate (see page 36), you can start to exercise the Pilates way whether you are male or female, young or old, and whether you are already fit or have not exercised for many years. Some examples of categories of people who can benefit from Pilates are illustrated here.

Older people
Pilates is a low impact form of exercise that is ideal for those with health problems or who have not exercised recently.

Young and fit
You can learn healthy patterns of movement and build strength and flexibility that will benefit you throughout life.

New mother
Once you are past the immediate postnatal period, Pilates exercise will help you regain tone in your abdominal muscles and pelvic floor.

Recovering from injury
Pilates exercise can help you regain strength and mobility after trauma such as broken bones and muscle strains.

Pilates and Other Therapies

Manipulative therapies

Many osteopaths and chiropractors recommend Pilates exercise as an adjunct to their treatments.

The Pilates approach to exercise was revolutionary at the time when it first became widely known. However, decades later, the experience of the thousands of people who have benefited from this system worldwide provides an irrefutable testimony to the effectiveness of the exercises. Many of Pilates' ideas have now been adopted by other fitness trainers and also by mainstream physiotherapy. Physicians often recommend Pilates exercise as part of a rehabilitation programme

following injury. With the agreement of your doctor, you can safely incorporate Pilates practice alongside most medical treatments. It is also widely recommended by osteopaths.

Similar therapies

Pilates has much in common with the Alexander Technique and the Feldenkrais Method. The founders of these systems, Frederick Alexander (1869–1955) and Moshe Feldenkrais (1904–84), were contemporaries of Joseph Pilates. Whether or not these bodywork pioneers knew each other personally, they drew on similar sources of inspiration. With their common emphasis on balanced body use, these exercise systems can be used together.

Body–mind therapies

Pilates was one of the first body–mind therapies to originate in the West. However, Eastern cultures have ancient traditions that recognize and build on the interaction between body and mind. Those who have practised forms of exercise such as yoga may find it easier to achieve the focus required than those who have never done so. Moreover, the emphasis on stretching is also common to both practices. Yet it is important to be aware of some basic differences between these systems, notably the breathing techniques recommended. Such differences can sometimes lead to conflict if both forms of exercise are used alongside each other.

Pilates Lifestyle

Joseph Pilates had his own views on the wider aspects of health and fitness, and made recommendations on topics as diverse as diet, bodily cleanliness (cold showers and skin scrubbing), and the benefits of exposure to sunshine. While many of his ideas still make sense today, others seem less relevant. Modern exponents of Pilates exercise do not necessarily follow all such recommendations. You do not have to take on board a rigid lifestyle programme in order to gain benefit from the Pilates exercise system.

PREPARING FOR PILATES

The Pilates exercises in this book are all based on matwork and therefore no specialized equipment or clothing is necessary. However, there are some important preliminaries that you will need to think about before embarking on this exercise programme. ✎ This chapter outlines the essential medical precautions you should take and the self-assessment body checks that should be carried out to identify any areas of weakness or misalignment that may need to be addressed in your programme.

Before You Start

Get advice
It is sensible to tell your medical practitioner if you plan to add Pilates exercise to a treatment programme.

Pilates aims to restore natural and healthy ways of using your body. In this sense it is a safe and suitable form of exercise for everyone. However, there are some basic, common-sense precautions you should take. It is always important to seek medical advice before starting any new exercise programme if you have a medical condition you are receiving treatment for. In addition, you should consult your doctor if you have not exercised regularly for several years or if you have suffered significant injury.

Pregnancy and childbirth

Avoid all Pilates exercise in the first 12 weeks of pregnancy. Some Pilates exercises are safe to do in the later stages, especially if you already have some experience of this form of exercise. But you should always seek medical advice and the guidance of a qualified Pilates teacher to help you devise a programme of exercises that is suitable for pregnancy. Pilates exercise is also a great way of getting back into shape after childbirth, but consult your doctor about when it is safe to start exercising before doing so.

When not to exercise

Effective practice of Pilates exercises depends on full engagement of body and mind. Any condition or factor that disrupts your ability to focus will make your practice less valuable and may incur the risk of injury. Do not exercise in any of the following circumstances:
• Within two hours of a meal.
• After drinking alcohol or taking mood-altering drugs such as tranquillizers.

Preparing for Pilates **Before You Start**

- You have a fever or feel unwell.
- You have suffered a recent injury.
- You have been taking over-the-counter or prescribed pain-relieving medication.

During exercise

To avoid strain and to gain maximum benefit, be careful to perform the exercises exactly as described. Do not exceed the number of repetitions advised, or progress to the more difficult exercises, until you are sure you have mastered the basics. As you perform each exercise it is normal to experience a stretching sensation in certain areas or to feel tiredness or aching in previously unused muscles. However, at no stage should you feel actual pain. If this occurs, discontinue the exercise and re-check the instructions; you may be getting something wrong. If you are unable to find the cause of the pain – that is, to discover any error you may be making, exclude that exercise from your routine until you are able to obtain the necessary guidance from an experienced Pilates teacher.

BODY CHARACTERISTICS

The first stage of body self-assessment is to teach yourself visual awareness of the ideal body alignment. This acts as a basis for comparison when you assess the alignment and other characteristics of your own body. The feet are the basis for our standing posture, so it is normal to check from the feet upwards. Look for the ideal characteristics illustrated on this page. Remember that none of us is perfect and that most of us deviate from the ideal in at least one or two respects.

Pelvis aligned – neither hip higher than the other

Knees facing forwards – neither bowed nor knock-kneed

Aiming for alignment
Pilates exercise aims to help you achieve symmetrical alignment of your shoulders and hips and of your head and neck over your spine. Such symmetry is not only pleasing to look at but also provides the basis for strain-free movement.

Feet in parallel facing forwards

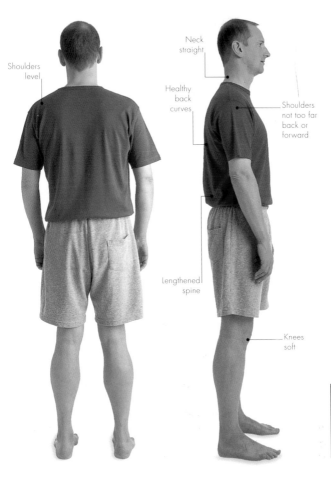

Shoulders
level

Neck
straight

Healthy
back
curves

Shoulders
not too far
back or
forward

Lengthened
spine

Knees
soft

Body Checks

Positioning
Your shoulders should be level and your hips aligned. Your head should be directly over your spine.

Ideal body alignment balances the heaviest areas of the body – head, ribcage, and pelvis – over one another to create maximum stability and minimum stress along the spine. Misalignment occurs when one of these elements shifts away from the centre – for example, if the head pokes forward, the spine tends to angle backwards to compensate. This stresses the muscles and ligaments of the spine, making injury more likely. It is common for a primary fault to create a succession of additional faults in an effort to redress the balance.

Head and neck

The head is, for its size, the heaviest part of the body. To avoid experiencing strain, its weight should be balanced evenly over the neck and spine, neither tipping to either side nor being held too far forward or back.

Shoulders

The shoulders should always appear to drop in a relaxed manner away from the neck. They should also align horizontally with one another. In profile the shoulders should be held neither too far forward nor too far back.

Curves of the back

We have already seen that the spine has both convex and concave curves when it is viewed in profile. These curves should not be flattened or exaggerated in any way.

Pelvis

The position of the pelvis is critical for good posture. In profile the pelvis should neither tip forwards excessively, which exaggerates the curve in the lower back, nor backwards, which over-flattens this curve. Pilates exercise teaches you to adopt a healthy, neutral position for the pelvis (see page 48).

Knees and legs

The position of the knees is in part determined by the alignment of the hip joint. The kneecaps should face directly forward and the knee joints should not angle inward (knock knees) or outward (bow legs). In profile the upper and lower legs should be aligned vertically between hips, knees, and ankles. If the lower leg curves back away from the vertical line then the knees are said to be hyperextended.

Ankles and feet

When standing, your feet should face directly forwards and carry your weight evenly across the soles of the feet.

IS THIS YOU?

The photographs on these pages illustrate some common postural faults. These may develop as a result of an inherited tendency or may be due to habitual poor posture. Pilates can help correct many of these faults, although it may mitigate rather than totally eliminate some problems. If you recognize your own faults here, do not be discouraged, but use the knowledge that you have corrective work to do to act as an incentive for your Pilates practice.

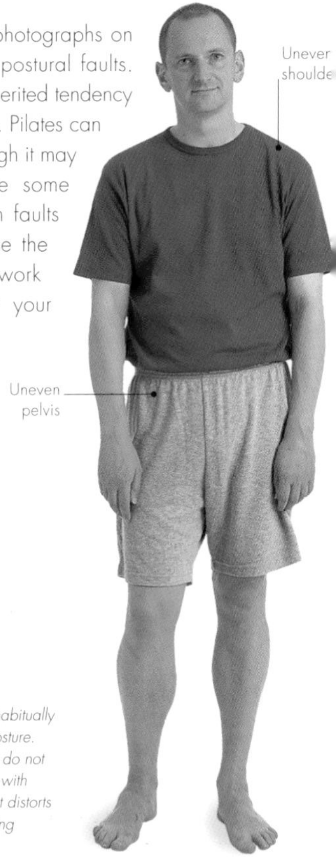

Uneven shoulders

Uneven pelvis

Common faults

Many, if not most of us habitually stand in a misaligned posture. Such "relaxed" positions do not in fact provide the body with rest, but create strain that distorts and stresses the supporting structures of the back.

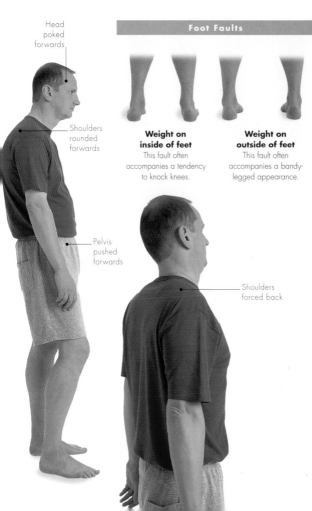

Head
poked
forwards

Foot Faults

Shoulders
rounded
forwards

**Weight on
inside of feet**
This fault often
accompanies a tendency
to knock knees.

**Weight on
outside of feet**
This fault often
accompanies a bandy-
legged appearance.

Pelvis
pushed
forwards

Shoulders
forced back

Clothes, Equipment, and Space

Clothing for comfort
Choose clothing for your Pilates practice that allows complete freedom of movement.

When you mention Pilates, some people immediately think of expensive fitness studios containing complicated exercise machines. It is true that some forms of Pilates exercise do use specially designed equipment. But matwork, the form of Pilates exercise with which this book is concerned, is wonderfully uncluttered and is therefore ideal for practising at home. There are, however, a few basic items that you will need in order to get the most out of your exercise sessions.

Clothes

It is a matter of common sense that you need to wear light garments, with no tight waistbands. In a class you may be encouraged to wear relatively close-fitting items, such as leotards, cycling shorts, and singlets. This is to allow the instructor to observe your body alignment and movements more closely. At home such considerations do not apply, although you may find it easier to judge the accuracy of your performance if you avoid large, baggy garments. Matwork exercises should be carried out without shoes.

Equipment

There are a few simple items that it is useful to have on hand:

• For some exercises you will need a long scarf or piece of fabric about 1m long x 20 centimetres wide (39 x 8 inches). If you prefer, you could buy a Dynaband from a sports supplier.

• A thin pillow or folded towel is useful to provide support for the head during floor exercises.

• Some form of padding for the floor surface is advised. You may want to obtain a purpose-made exercise mat, but you can easily improvise with a thick rug or a folded blanket.

• Eventually you may reach the stage where you want to use weights to increase the challenge of the exercises.

Space

Pilates exercise can be practised in any space large enough for you to lie down with your arms outstretched. For preference, choose a warm but well-ventilated room with a non-slip floor surface in a part of the home where you won't be disturbed.

RE-EDUCATING BODY AND MIND

You are now familiar with the principles of Pilates, so are ready to get down to some practical work. In this chapter you will be focusing on mastering each of the basic techniques that underpin all Pilates exercise. Don't skimp on this section or you will find that your progress through the foundation exercises in the next chapter will be impaired. At the end of this chapter you will also find advice on how to plan and schedule your exercise sessions in order to achieve balanced results.

Alignment

Checklist
Do a mental checklist to ensure that all parts of your body are aligned.

In chapter two we looked at some aspects of body alignment. Each time you commence an exercise session, it is important to establish a well-aligned posture. At first you may need to make many adjustments, but your body will learn these new habits of alignment and therefore will fall into place more easily.

Supine alignment

The body, in particular the spine, is at its most relaxed when lying down on the back in what is called the supine position. It is therefore best to begin your posture adjustment in this position. For this introduction to the Pilates routine, it is helpful to have someone to observe and correct you. Obviously, if you are in a class, your teacher will do this for you. If you are exercising at home, persuade a family member or friend to help you. Brief them on the key features that you are trying to achieve and ask them to let you know when you have got it right.

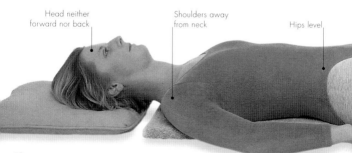

Head neither forward nor back

Shoulders away from neck

Hips level

Key alignment points

Lie down on your padded surface, supporting your head with a flat pillow or folded towel if necessary. Working from feet to head, check the following:

• Your feet and knees are hip-width apart, facing forward, and parallel.

• Your hips are level.

• Your arms are resting a short distance from your sides; palms may be up or down, elbows are slightly bent.

• Your shoulders are level and relaxing away from your neck.

• Your neck is lengthened.

• Your head is not tilted forward or rolling back.

Neutral pelvis

Viewed from the side the pelvis should be held in a way that maintains the normal concave curve of the lower back at the waist – the lumbar curve. If the pelvis tips forward, the lumbar curve is exaggerated; if it tips back, the curve is flattened. Either of these positions can create back strain if it forms part of your habitual posture. The exact position of neutral pelvis is different for each individual. Locating the neutral position for your pelvis in the supine position will be among your first Pilates tasks.

Knees forward and parallel

Feet forward and parallel

ALIGNMENT EXERCISES

On the previous pages you were instructed how to adjust your basic body alignment in the supine position. Here, you will take this further and begin to learn how to relax and enhance your awareness of your body alignment. Of particular importance is the procedure for locating the neutral position for your pelvis. This preparatory relaxation routine can be used as your regular starter exercise before performing other Pilates exercises. Some people like to play relaxation tapes during this exercise.

1 *From the basic supine position described on the previous pages, bend your knees and place your feet flat on the floor hip-width apart. Be aware of the equal distribution of weight between the centre of the heel and the outer and inner parts of the ball of each foot. Feel your body relaxing into the floor, your muscles softening and your spine lengthening. Allow your spine to adopt a natural position. Visualize your shoulder blades relaxing down your back, but do not force any movement. Also relax your jaw and facial muscles.*

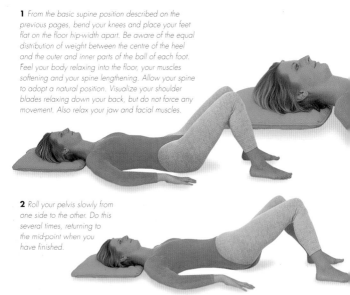

2 *Roll your pelvis slowly from one side to the other. Do this several times, returning to the mid-point when you have finished.*

3 After a few moments of relaxation, tilt your pelvis forward so that your pubic bone moves downwards and the hollow between your lower spine and the floor increases. Keep the rest of your body and your legs relaxed as you do this.

From Above

4 Next, tilt your pelvis back by drawing your navel towards your spine and lifting the pubic bone so that the hollow in your back flattens and there is no longer any space between your lower back and the floor.

Throughout all of these exercises, keep your pelvis aligned horizontally, with your feet in line with your knees and hips.

5 Now return to a relaxed mid-point between these two extremes, in which the pelvis is level, neither tipping forward nor back. There should be a slight gap between your lower back and the floor. This is your neutral pelvis position. Repeat steps 3 to 5 five times.

The Pelvic Floor

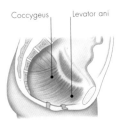

Coccygeus   Levator ani

Pelvic floor muscles
*These internal muscles
provide vital support for the
organs within the pelvis.*

When we refer to the centring muscles, this not only includes the familiar "stomach" muscles at the front of the abdomen, but it also involves the hammock of muscles that holds the internal organs within the pelvis. Although the pelvis does vary between men and women (in women it's shallower and broader) it is vital for all of us to be aware of our pelvic floor and to exercise its muscles. These muscles are among the most important centring muscles of all but many people are unaware of their existence, let alone how to bring them into active use.

Pelvic floor muscles

The pelvic floor is a mesh of muscles and ligaments that extends from the pubic bone at the front of the pelvis, passes under the pelvic opening between the legs, and joins to the base of the spine. These muscles surround and control the neck of the bladder and the urethra (outlet from the bladder), the anus, and – in women – the vagina.

Why are they important?

When they are toned and active the pelvic floor muscles provide strong support for the pelvic organs, including the bladder, and uterus (women) or prostate (men), during physical activity. They also help to provide control of urination and defecation. If your pelvic floor muscles are slack – as a result of lack of use, obesity, or childbirth – you risk developing stress incontinence (leakage of urine when pressure within the abdomen is increased, such as during exertion or coughing). There is also a greater likelihood of prolapse of the internal organs.

In Pilates terms, the pelvic floor muscles are the lowest part of the girdle of strength that stabilizes and strengthens the torso as a whole, which is why you will be required to align them in the "neutral pelvis" position at the beginning of many Pilates exercises. These muscles are also extremely important for initiating the toning of the postural muscles deep within the abdomen. The need for balance in your physical training dictates that all of the centring muscles are developed to the same degree, otherwise you will not achieve the harmonious results that you are seeking. For these reasons, be sure to build pelvic floor exercises into your regular exercise routine.

Not Just for Women

Many people believe that slack pelvic floor muscles are a purely female problem. This is far from the truth. Men need to maintain a firm pelvic floor as well. Many of the urinary problems that men may suffer in middle age and beyond can be ameliorated by toning the pelvic floor.

ENGAGING THE PELVIC FLOOR

The following exercise should be a regular part of your Pilates routine. The movement is hard to see in a photograph or when demonstrated by someone else; you really have to try it yourself and learn what it feels like. Once you have learned to recognize the sensation of tightening the pelvic floor you can practise this movement anytime, anywhere. The main technique you need to try to master is that of keeping the buttocks and abdominal muscles relaxed while you engage those of the pelvic floor – but this is always a challenge.

1 *Lie on the floor with your knees bent and your feet on the floor (see also step 1, page 50). Engage the muscles of the pelvic floor as if you were trying to stop urinating mid-stream. As you do this, place one hand on your buttocks to check that you have not also tightened your buttock muscles. Hold for as long you can, breathing normally throughout.*

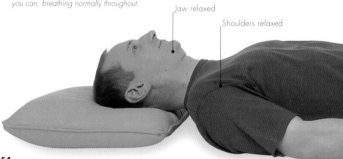

Jaw relaxed

Shoulders relaxed

2 In the same position, engage the pelvic floor muscles again. This time place your hand on your lower abdomen, just above the pubic bone, to check that you are not over-gripping the abdominal muscles or the muscles at the front of the thighs at the same time. When you are able to isolate your pelvic floor muscles, repeat the exercise five more times, holding for a minimum of ten seconds each time.

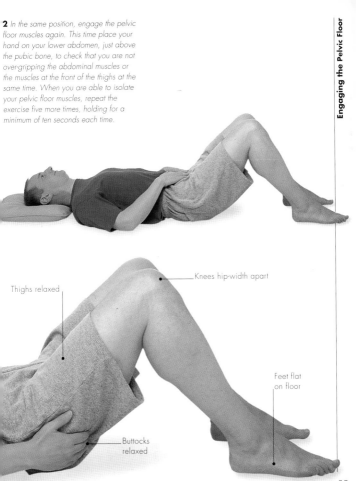

Thighs relaxed

Knees hip-width apart

Feet flat on floor

Buttocks relaxed

Engaging the Mind

Body image
Think of your body as a movable
model to help you visualize the
movements you should make.

O ne of the key characteristics of
Pilates exercise is that it aims
to enhance conscious control
of the body. In naming his exercise
system Contrology, Joseph Pilates was
emphasizing the importance of this
mental aspect of the exercises. He
attached great importance to his
perception that most people carry out
physical actions without any conscious
direction from the brain, operating on
an automatic level that reinforces
habitual movements that are not
necessarily beneficial to posture or

health. He described the effect of
bringing greater control into the
physical actions of the body as a
reawakening of thousands of brain
cells. Modern neurologists may question
the accuracy of this premise in actual
physical terms, but those who practise
Pilates exercise with the full degree of
mental engagement envisaged do in
fact testify to an increased sense of
alertness and mental energy.

The power of self-belief

One of the first mental challenges you
will meet is the initial difficulty you will
almost certainly encounter when trying
even the simplest exercises for the first
time. Co-ordinating your breathing
technique with the correct use of
particular muscles is not easy for any
newcomer to Pilates.

At this early stage you need to bring
to bear a sense of commitment to the
process of learning a new discipline
and also a belief in your own power
to improve. You must accept that
enhancing your control over your body

s a long-term project, but you should
have confidence that it is one in which
you will ultimately succeed.

Techniques for mental focus

Body awareness is a "two-way street" –
as well as learning to give accurate
instructions to the muscles of your
body, you also need to develop
your sensitivity to the sensations and
messages that they send back to your
brain. To focus effectively on the muscle
actions of the body you need to
eliminate all distractions. Apart from
taking the obvious practical steps to
minimize potential outside interruptions,
such as telephone calls, you will benefit
from developing your inner powers
of concentration, too. Many people
find that their concentration benefits
enormously from practising some form
of meditation. There are numerous
techniques that you can try, from simple
breathing meditations to more elaborate
visualization methods. Some basic
visualization exercises are described
on the following pages.

Model motion
Visualization can aid concentration, thus helping you attain the correct body movement.

VISUALIZATIONS
In Pilates most people find that their grasp of the exercises is improved if they use visualizations to help them picture the movement they are trying to create. Each person's imagination works in a different way but the visualizations on this page are useful for most people.

Pelvic stability
To help you anchor your pelvis while performing abdominal curls and similar exercises, imagine that the area from your pubic bone to the bottom of the ribcage is set in concrete.

Lengthening
In the supine position you need to keep a sense of lengthening through the spine. Prevent tension from creeping into this action by visualizing a cord attached to the top of your head that is gently stretching your head and neck away from your body. Imagine another cord similarly pulling your tailbone towards your feet.

Curling the spine

Several exercises, including the spine lift (see pages 86–87), ask you to curl and uncurl the spine. It is important to maintain a sense of lifting as well as curling and to imagine each vertebra lifting up separately from the floor as you do this. You could visualize the process as seeing the sprockets of a gear wheel disengaging link by link from a chain.

Navel to spine

One way to picture this fundamental action is to imagine a piece of string attached to your navel running through your body and emerging from your spine at the back. When you draw your navel to your spine it is as if someone were pulling this string to bring your navel closer to your backbone.

Breathing

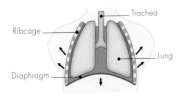

Inspiration
When you breathe in, the diaphragm flattens and the ribcage expands.

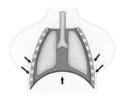

Expiration
When you breathe out, the diaphragm domes and the ribcage contracts.

When we breathe we are taking in oxygen, one of the vital ingredients that the body needs to produce energy for movement and other functions. Efficient breathing is therefore a prerequisite for optimum physical performance and it is easy to understand why Joseph Pilates emphasized the importance of breathing correctly.

Thoracic breathing

Some forms of deep breathing involve distending the abdomen as you inhale. This is not recommended in Pilates as it allows excessive relaxation of the abdominal muscles, which is not desirable during exercise because it leads to instability at the "centre". The breathing technique that is taught for Pilates exercise is known as thoracic or rib breathing. In this method you aim to keep your abdominals and other centring muscles engaged while your ribcage expands with the "in-breath". Your shoulders should remain relaxed and should not hunch up as you inhale. On the "out-breath" the ribcage contracts down towards the waist and expels the waste air. During the out-breath you should be aware of all your centring muscles, including the pelvic floor, being actively engaged and drawing towards the centre.

Breathing sequence

In almost every Pilates exercise you
inhale before initiating a movement.
Then as you begin to exhale, start the
exercise. In an exercise involving more
than one movement element, you may
be required to pause and take an in-
breath before completing the exercise
on a second out-breath. Moving on the
out-breath helps you to engage your
centring muscles throughout the exercise
and prevents any build up of unwanted
tension. This breathing method also
helps you avoid "doming" of the
abdominals during curl-ups (see pages
102–103), which can lead to the
development of a bulging abdomen.

Body Release

To help dispel tension in the muscles and
joints, lie down in the supine position (see
pages 48–49) and breathe steadily. Imagine
that each in-breath is drawing air into your
body through the soles of your feet. As the
breath moves through the legs and into the
torso it softly envelops the joints and muscles,
releasing any stiffness.

BREATHING EXERCISES

It is very worthwhile practising rib breathing as a separate exercise every time you do a Pilates workout until you are confident that you have thoroughly mastered the technique. It may seem strange at first to be inhaling while your lower abdomen is pulled in, but you will soon find that this way of breathing starts to come naturally. In the exercise shown here your hands should be placed on your ribcage to help heighten your awareness of the expansion and contraction of the ribcage as you breathe. Some Pilates teachers recommend wrapping a long scarf around your ribcage during breathing practice as another way of achieving this. Use whatever method works best for you but always ensure you perform this exercise in front of a mirror.

1 *Place your hands, fingertips touching, on your ribs.*

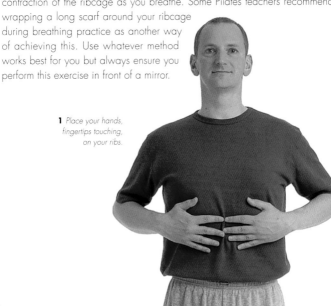

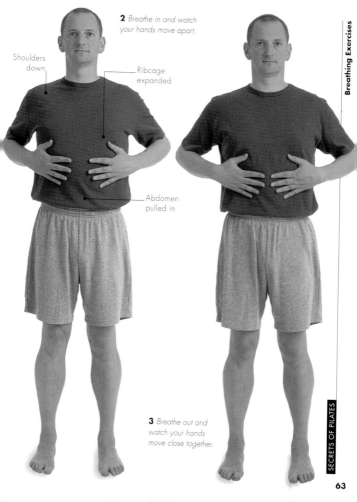

2 *Breathe in and watch your hands move apart.*

Shoulders down

Ribcage expanded

Abdomen pulled in

3 *Breathe out and watch your hands move close together.*

Rest and Relaxation

Kneeling rest position
This relaxation position is most useful after strenuous extension exercises for the back (see page 122).

Effort and relaxation are two sides of the same coin; you cannot have one without the other. If you do not use your muscles, you cannot appreciate the benefits of relaxation; if you never relax, then your muscles will not work to their optimum capacity. Because of this, every effective exercise programme builds in a phase of relaxation and the Pilates method is no exception. You must set a few minutes aside for relaxation at the end of each practice, in order to allow any tension that was built up during your exercise session to drain away. This will enable your body to assimilate the benefits of the activities before you resume your everyday routine.

Specific relaxation

For many Pilates exercises there is a complementary relaxation position that you can adopt following a workout that specifically rests the muscles that you have just been using. For example, after doing curl-ups, which work the abdominal muscles, it is important to rest these muscles by clasping your knees to your chest for a few moments (see page 103). The kneeling rest position (see page 122) gently stretches out the entire spine after doing back extension exercises.

Not only do these complementary positions provide the opportunity for a welcome rest after strenuous exercise, they also lengthen the muscles that have been working, thereby preventing loss of flexibility that can sometimes accompany repeated contraction of a group of muscles. For these reasons, it is important not to skimp on the relaxation elements of your Pilates routine; they are integral to your programme and just as important as the main exercises themselves.

General relaxation

When you have completed your exercise programme, adopt the neutral pelvis position (see pages 50–51). Rest in this way for a few minutes and consciously allow any sign of tension to ebb away into the floor. You could also take up the relaxation position shown on page 207. Alternatively, adopt the kneeling rest position shown left, focusing all your attention on your breathing as you do so.

Pilates and Sleep

Pilates saw his exercise method as a route to all-round health and well-being. While modern Pilates teachers tend to limit their advice to the exercise aspect of Pilates teaching, there is no doubt that performing exercise regularly has a beneficial impact on sleep quality and, conversely, that your sleep patterns can affect your Pilates performance. A body that is tired through physical exertion will achieve sound sleep more easily than one that has been physically sedentary but mentally tense. Regular sleep of sufficient duration (most of us need about seven hours a night) provides a firm foundation for physical performance, particularly of the controlled type of exercise practised in Pilates.

PROGRAMME PLANNER

This suggested exercise programme is designed to provide a balanced seven-day programme of foundation exercises – designed to be repeated at least once – to teach and build basic strength and skills. Each session starts with breathing and alignment exercises and includes mobilization exercises, hamstring and quad stretches, and a wind-down. You can adapt the elements if you want to, provided you maintain a balance between different types of exercises: flexion/extension, stretches/strengthening.

Day	Group 1	Group 2	Group 3
1	Alignment exercises (page 50) with Breathing exercises (page 62)	Head and neck rolls (page 74) Shoulder mobilization (page 78)	Spine lift (page 86)
2	Alignment exercises (page 50) with Breathing exercises (page 62)	Head and neck rolls (page 74) Shoulder mobilization (page 78)	Knee lifts and drops (page 94)
3	Alignment exercises (page 50) with Breathing exercises (page 62)	Head and neck rolls (page 74) Shoulder mobilization (page 78)	Inner thigh squeeze (page 82)
4	Active standing (page 126) with Breathing exercises (page 62)	Head and neck rolls (page 74) Doming and toe wriggling (page 135)	Pedalling (page 138)
5	Alignment exercises (page 50) with Breathing exercises (page 62)	Head and neck rolls (page 74) Shoulder mobilization (page 78)	Spine lift (page 86)
6	Alignment exercises (page 50) with Breathing exercises (page 62)	Head and neck rolls (page 74) Shoulder mobilization (page 78)	Knee lifts and drops (page 94)
7	Active standing (page 126) with Breathing exercises (page 62)	Head and neck rolls (page 74) Doming and toe wriggling (page 135)	Ankle rotations, pointing and flexing (page 134)

Tips for Practice

If you feel tired or under the weather either skip your practice or do a reduced version that is limited to mobilizations and stretches. You can always return to a foundation version of any exercise if you feel overworked.

If you can't practise every day, don't worry: practise when you can, but remember you will progress more slowly.

Group 4	Group 5	Group 6	Group 7
Abdominal curls (page 102)	Back extension (page 106) and rest position (page 122)	Quad stretches (page 118) Hamstring stretches (page 98)	Chest opening (page 202)
Hip rolls (page 50)	Prone inner thigh squeeze (page 114)	Quad stretches (page 118) Hamstring stretches (page 98)	Full body stretches (page 206)
Abdominal curls (page 102)	Back extension (page 106) and rest position (page 122)	Quad stretches (page 118) Hamstring stretches (page 98)	Roll downs (page 130)
Roll downs (page 130)	Ankle rotations, pointing and flexing (page 134)	Quad stretches (page 118) Hamstring stretches (page 98)	Full body stretches (page 206)
Hip rolls (page 50)	Back extension (page 106) and rest position (page 122)	Quad stretches (page 118) Hamstring stretches (page 98)	Chest opening (page 202)
Abdominal curls (page 102)	Prone leg stretch (page 110)	Quad stretches (page 118) Hamstring stretches (page 98)	Breathing practice in the rest position (page 122)
Knee lifts and drops (page 94)	Prone inner thigh squeeze (page 114)	Quad stretches (page 118) Hamstring stretches (page 98)	Roll downs (page 130)

Your Personal Programme

Self-discipline
You will need to engage your mental powers to stick to your planned exercise programme.

The exercise programme on the previous pages is designed to provide a balanced structure to your practice. Although it is based around a seven-day sequence, you can practise on alternate days if your daily routine does not allow for more frequent sessions. You will still progress, albeit more slowly. Repeat the seven-day sequence at least once before thinking about extending your practice.

Longer sessions

The daily programme is designed to be short, because most people don't have time for a long session every day. If you have time and energy you can add extra foundation exercises to your programme. But make sure that you practise all the exercises equally and do not overtire yourself – this may ultimately be counterproductive. With longer practice you may build your strength more effectively, but it is still advisable to spend a minimum of 14 days on your foundation programme. This gives your body the chance to assimilate the new habits you are teaching it.

Preparing to progress

After 14 days of practice, you may wish to review your progress. Read the self-assessment guidelines on page 140 before deciding to progress. If you feel confident that you are ready to extend your practice, add one of the additional exercises listed in the box to your daily practice. When you feel that you have mastered a foundation exercise, you can then substitute its progressed version. It's probably best not to include more than one new exercise in any one session – integrate new exercises into your programme gradually.

Additional Exercises

The following progression exercises can be added to your programme when you feel that you are ready

Four-square breathing (page 146)

Turned-out knee raises (page 162)

Arm raises and rotations (page 186)

The Spring (page 190)

Seated side stretches and rotations (page 194)

Side leg lifts (page 198)

Choosing Your Progression Exercise

Foundation exercise	Progression
Spine lift (page 86)	Spine lift with overhead stretch (page 151)
Abdominal curls (page 102)	Progressed abdominal curls (page 166) The Hundred (page 170) Diagonal shoulder raise (page 174)
Back extension (page 106)	The Javelin (page 182)
Hip rolls (page 50)	Double knee lift and roll (page 154)
Prone leg stretch (page 110)	Diagonal stretch variations (page 178)
Prone inner thigh squeeze (page 114)	The Javelin (page 182)
Roll downs (page 130)	The Spring (page 190)
Hamstring stretches (page 98)	Seated hamstring stretches (page 158)

FOUNDATION
EXERCISES

The exercises in this chapter provide a sound foundation for any newcomer to Pilates. They act as a warm-up as well as a gentle introduction to the strengthening and realignment of the body, which is the ultimate aim of your Pilates journey. Don't expect to master all of these exercises straight away. It may take several weeks of practice to perform them all with confidence, and you certainly won't have time to complete more than a small proportion of them in a single session. Remember to vary your programme to include all of the exercises on a regular basis. Every body has its own strengths and weaknesses, so it is normal to find some exercises easier than others. Remember to read the cautions outlined on page 36 before you start.

Mobilizing the Neck

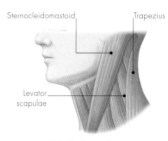

Principal muscles
The neck is supported and mobilized by muscles that connect the skull, vertebrae, collar bone, and shoulder blades.

Pilates exercise encourages you to create a long neck that is able to support the weight of the head in a completely balanced way. This improves your appearance, reduces strain on the neck muscles and bones (cervical vertebrae), and contributes to the overall alignment of the spine.

The neck muscles

The muscles that are involved in moving the neck are:

• The sternocleidomastoid, which is the prominent muscle that runs from the ear to the front of the base of the neck. This muscle enables you to turn your head and pull it forwards.

• The trapezius, which is attached to the top of the spine at one end and to the shoulder blade at the other. This lifts the shoulder.

• The levator scapulae, which is attached to the vertebrae in the neck and to the shoulder blade. This stabilizes the shoulder blade.

Neck stiffness

Each of the neck muscles easily becomes tense and stiff in people who have stressful, sedentary jobs. Once you are aware of this problem, it is easy to catch yourself bringing your shoulders up towards your ears at times of anxiety or concentration. Neck tension in turn leads to hunching of the shoulders and may be a contributory factor in recurrent headaches and back pain. Mobilizing your neck muscles helps to rid yourself of such tension and the problems it causes. Releasing neck tension can help to improve posture and relieve recurrent aches and pains.

Releasing the neck

In order to start using the neck muscles correctly, you first need to release any tension they may be holding, as this may restrict or distort your freedom of movement. The exercises shown on the following pages are performed in the supine (lying down) position. This allows you gently to stretch and mobilize the neck muscles in a position where they do not need to support the weight of the head. Make sure that you perform these movements slowly and with concentration, as rapid movement of the head and neck carries the risk of muscle strain and possible stress on the joints and cushioning discs between the neck vertebrae.

Take Care

If, when you try the neck exercises, you find that moving your neck causes dizziness, faintness, pain, numbness, or tingling in the arm or hand you should stop the exercise immediately and seek medical advice. The movement may have been compressing a nerve or blood vessel in the neck.

HEAD AND NECK ROLLS

These simple movements are a relaxing preamble to the more challenging exercises. Perform them in the supine position after you have rested in the neutral pelvis position for a few moments. As with many Pilates exercises, you must not be deceived by the apparent simplicity of the movement required. You need to concentrate and engage your powers of body awareness to be sure that your exercise is having the effect that it should. Make sure that you breathe naturally and easily throughout the exercise.

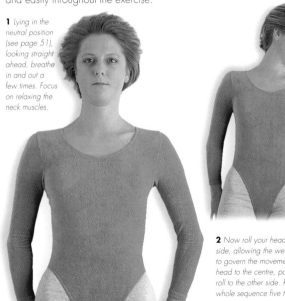

1 Lying in the neutral position (see page 51), looking straight ahead, breathe in and out a few times. Focus on relaxing the neck muscles.

2 Now roll your head slowly to one side, allowing the weight of the head to govern the movement. Return your head to the centre, pause, and then roll to the other side. Repeat the whole sequence five times.

3 *From the starting position, raise your chin to tilt your head backwards.*

4 *Now bring your chin towards your chest so that you feel a gentle stretch in the back of the neck. Slowly repeat steps 3 and 4 five times.*

5 *Return to the starting position and breathe easily for a few moments.*

Shoulder Release

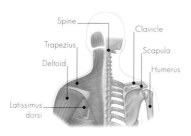

Shoulder structures

The muscles involved in movement of the shoulders are attached to the spine, shoulder blade (scapula), collar bone (clavicle) and/or upper arm bone (humerus).

Once you have released the neck area, the next step is to start the process of freeing and realigning the shoulders. We have already seen how tension can be focused in both the neck and shoulders. At times of mental and emotional stress the shoulder muscles tighten and over time become shortened, which pulls the upper body out of alignment. Hunched and rounded shoulders limit the expansion of the chest and therefore have a restrictive effect on breathing.

Add to this the problems caused by crouching for long periods over a desk that may be the wrong height, and the strain and long-term distortion caused by carrying heavy loads such as bags of shopping or a heavy briefcase – always in the same hand – and the result is one in which free and balanced movement of the upper body and arms is a virtual impossibility. However, it's possible to get your shoulders back to how they should be.

Benefits of shoulder release

In Pilates it is a key axiom that the shoulders should always be relaxed downward. When you hold your shoulders correctly in this way your entire spine, from neck to pelvis, lengthens. The ribcage is also freed up, which allows greater expansion of the lungs and therefore creates more effective breathing. When the shoulders are mobile and stabilized through appropriate exercise, the range of movement of the arms is increased and the risk of strain is reduced.

Visual indicators

The tops of the shoulders can be seen easily if you look into a mirror, so it is relatively straightforward to spot when they are hunching up towards your ears or if one is raised higher than the other. A few shrugs that allow the shoulders to drop down from the ears will often help to release this area.

You are probably less aware, however, of the position of your shoulder blades. When you are tense these tend to ride up the back, which contributes to a round-shouldered appearance. When realigning the shoulders, a prime consideration is to develop a sense of the shoulder blades "sliding down" the back towards your waist. Once you have taught yourself to recognize when this is happening, you should make it your mission to remind yourself to keep your shoulder blades dropped at all times. Try checking every ten minutes or so to see if your shoulder blades are still in a dropped position – you will soon come to recognize how to tell if they start riding up again.

SHOULDER MOBILIZATION

The initial exercise for adjusting the shoulders is a simple, vertical arm stretch and dropping movement, which eases out tension and allows the newly relaxed shoulder to fall back into a more natural position. The exercise then progresses to an overhead stretch. All of this is done in the supine position, which helps to support the rest of the body while you focus on the shoulders. Rest your head on a folded towel or thin pillow if you wish.

1 Lying in the neutral position with your arms at your sides, visualize your body lengthening without strain, from head to toe. Breathe into the ribs and as you breathe out raise your arms vertically with the palms facing each other. Stretch your arms up as if you were being pulled by your fingertips, but keep your elbows soft.

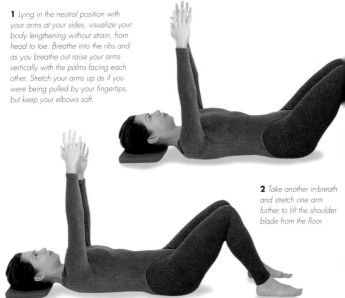

2 Take another in-breath and stretch one arm further to lift the shoulder blade from the floor.

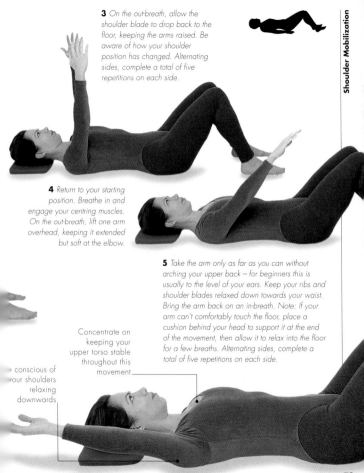

3 On the out-breath, allow the shoulder blade to drop back to the floor, keeping the arms raised. Be aware of how your shoulder position has changed. Alternating sides, complete a total of five repetitions on each side.

4 Return to your starting position. Breathe in and engage your centring muscles. On the out-breath, lift one arm overhead, keeping it extended but soft at the elbow.

5 Take the arm only as far as you can without arching your upper back – for beginners this is usually to the level of your ears. Keep your ribs and shoulder blades relaxed down towards your waist. Bring the arm back on an in-breath. Note: If your arm can't comfortably touch the floor, place a cushion behind your head to support it at the end of the movement, then allow it to relax into the floor for a few breaths. Alternating sides, complete a total of five repetitions on each side.

Concentrate on keeping your upper torso stable throughout this movement

conscious of your shoulders relaxing downwards

79

Isolating the Inner Thigh

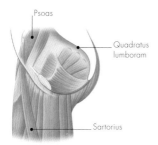

Psoas

Quadratus lumboram

Sartorius

Inner thigh muscles

These important muscles need to be both strong and free from stiffness to allow ease of leg movement.

Learning to identify separate groups of muscles, and mastering how to use them independently, is an important aspect of Pilates that is known as isolation. Most of us use our bodies without any consciousness of the precise muscles that we are engaging in the course of any movement. We operate on the basis of automatic and habitual patterns of movement that scarcely impinge on our thought processes. And it is often true that the muscles used in our movements are not those that are the most efficient for that action, or that we actually use muscles that are unnecessary and therefore create needless tiredness.

As you become proficient in Pilates, your awareness of the actions of your body will increase and you will learn how to control your movements to bring the muscles you want to use into play for any particular action that you wish to undertake. As a result, your movements will become more economical, harmonious, and graceful. You will also be less prone to injury because your actions will be less haphazard. You will be much more in control of your body and what happens to it as you move around.

Inner thigh and pelvic floor

Among the muscle groups that many of us have lost conscious control over – with the result that they are underused – are those of the inner thigh and pelvic floor. When asked to engage them, most of us have a tendency to tense the entire buttock area as well, which counters the spine-lengthening and pelvis-stabilizing benefits of using just the pelvic floor and inner thigh. The exercise on pages 82–83 is designed to exercise these often-neglected muscles specifically. Because of the difficulty most people experience in working these muscles, the exercise is also valuable for improving focus, concentration, and body awareness.

The exercise is intended to work the lower part of the girdle of strength. When you are starting Pilates it is easy for strenuous physical effort to create tension in the upper back and shoulders as you attempt to bring your whole body into the exercise – it is important that you learn to relax. Throughout this exercise constantly remind yourself that the upper body, shoulders, and neck should be relaxed and check for signs of tension regularly in your jaw, neck, and shoulders (see page 77). The groin and fronts of the thighs are other areas where unwanted tension can build up. Check that these areas are relaxed and are kept "soft" throughout the exercise.

Rolled towel
Use a firmly rolled towel for this exercise, if you don't have a suitable cushion.

INNER THIGH SQUEEZE

For this exercise you will need a firm cushion or a rolled towel that you will place between your knees and squeeze. It is important that you start the exercise lying with your pelvis in a neutral position (see pages 48–51), and your shoulder blades relaxed downward, and that you employ a general sense of lengthening down the entire spine. The exercise itself may seem simple at first, but it takes time and practice to perfect the art of working only the muscles that are required. Recheck your technique at each repetition. There should be no tension in your upper body or buttocks.

1 *Lie in the neutral position with your knees bent and your feet together, flat on the floor. Place a cushion or rolled towel between your knees.*

2 *Breathe in. On the out-breath engage the pelvic floor, hollow your tummy, and squeeze the cushion between your knees using only your inner thigh muscles. Aim to hold this squeeze and control your out-breath for a count of ten. Repeat the exercise six times.*

No tension in upper body

Knees and Feet Together

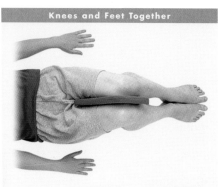

Viewed from above, you can see the knees, ankles, and feet are kept close together. Don't allow the legs to shift out of alignment during this exercise. If the leg alignment shifts, the pelvis will in turn also move out of alignment.

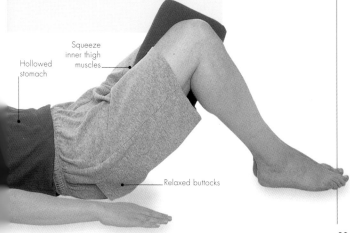

Squeeze inner thigh muscles

Hollowed stomach

Relaxed buttocks

Mobilizing the Lower Back

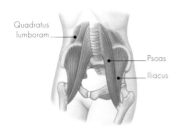

Quadratus
lumboram

Psoas

Iliacus

Internal abdominal muscles
*Pilates back and abdominal
exercises help to tone and
strengthen these muscles.*

By the time we reach adulthood most of us have lost much of the spinal mobility that we enjoyed as children. A sedentary lifestyle without a range of physical activities usually results in stiff muscles and ligaments in the back. Such stiffness makes us more prone to injury and can lead to chronic back problems. Even those who lead a more physically active life, such as sportspeople or those who are engaged in some form of physical work, often use their backs in an unbalanced way that creates strain on the structures of the back.

Weak abdominals, weak back

A reduced range of movement in the spine is almost always accompanied by a weakness in the abdominal muscles. Active abdominal muscles control and protect the spine during movement as well as when we are sitting or standing. For this reason, Pilates exercises that are specifically aimed at benefitting the back always involve the abdominal and other centring muscles too.

From pelvic tilt to spine lift

As part of the alignment exercises on pages 50–51, you learned to position your pelvis in relation to the spine to create a neutral position. The spine lift exercise on the following pages builds on this awareness of the alignment of your pelvis and lower back, and helps you to create and control a healthy range of movement in this area. The emphasis here is on locating and using your balanced, neutral position for your pelvis – remember this is different for everyone – and then learning to use your centring muscles to maintain that position while engaging in a range of movements. To achieve this it is important to follow the instructions carefully and to build up the number of repetitions gradually. You need to take time now to ensure that you find the correct position to undertake each of the foundation exercises: one repetition well executed is worth far more than a full number completed incorrectly.

The Power of Visualization

Remember that visualization techniques can be an invaluable aid in the correct practice of Pilates exercises. Everyone needs to develop their own visual vocabulary – an image that helps one person does not necessarily help another (see page 58). In the spine lift exercise shown on pages 86–87, use whatever image works best for you.

SPINE LIFT

No matter how long you have been practising Pilates, there is always a benefit in returning to the basics periodically. Checking and rechecking the alignment of your pelvis and spine is one of these basic exercises and you will encounter it as a recurring element in many of the exercises throughout this book. The spine lift is designed to reinforce correct pelvic positioning and to help you build the strength in your centring muscles needed to maintain that alignment when you are moving as well as when static. In this exercise, spinal mobility and lengthening are combined with stability at the centre.

1 *Lie down with your knees bent and your feet flat on the floor, hip-width apart. Rest your arms at your sides.*

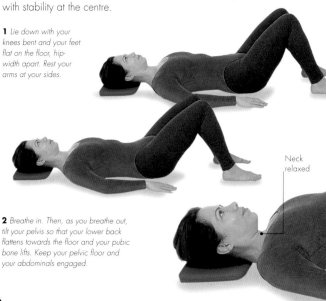

Neck relaxed

2 *Breathe in. Then, as you breathe out, tilt your pelvis so that your lower back flattens towards the floor and your pubic bone lifts. Keep your pelvic floor and your abdominals engaged.*

3 As you breathe out, tilt your pelvis in the opposite direction to increase the curve in your lower back. Keep your pelvic floor and your abdominals engaged. Then return to the neutral position. Repeat this process a few times to establish a sense of where your neutral position is.

4 In your neutral position, breathe in. As you breathe out, engage your pelvic floor and hollow your abdomen just enough to curl your tailbone off the floor. Do this by imagining each vertebra in turn, from tailbone to upper back, peeling up from the floor. Try to keep your thigh muscles relaxed and your weight supported equally between your feet throughout.

5 Stop when you have lifted to the point where your thighs and torso are in a straight line and you are resting on your shoulder blades. Hold the position and take an in-breath without relaxing the centring muscles. Then, as you breathe out, reverse the movement, slowly lowering each vertebra in turn onto the floor to return to your starting position. Use your centring muscles to control your body during the entire exercise.

Centring muscles engaged

Rotating the Spine

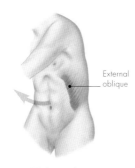

External oblique

Waist work

Working the external oblique muscles helps to strengthen and tone the waist area.

In the previous exercise on pages 86–87 the focus was on mobilizing the lower spine to create more flexibility and strength by bending it forwards (flexion) and backwards (extension). However, the spine also has the potential to rotate on a horizontal plane (see diagram above). This flexibility of movement allows the upper body to turn to the side while the pelvic area remains stable and front-facing.

Benefits of rotational strength

By controlling and strengthening this rotating movement you can again provide protection against back injuries that commonly occur as a result of excessive twisting of the spine, which can happen when such a movement is unsupported by strong centring muscles. Common activities, such as turning to lift a bag of shopping or to reach a jar in a kitchen cupboard, can easily lead to back strain if you haven't learned to protect your spine by using the whole range of abdominal muscles that are available to you.

Exercises that rotate the spine are particularly important as they release tension in the middle back and stretch out the muscles of the sides and waist area. This part of the back often becomes compressed during long periods of sitting and therefore exercises that mobilize it often provide immediate benefits in terms of relieving minor aches and stiffness. By learning how to rotate your spine you should notice your body becoming less stiff very quickly.

Multi-purpose exercise

Few exercises in Pilates have a single purpose, and rotational work for the spine is no exception. In addition to mobilizing and stretching the back, you will also be developing your oblique abdominal muscles as they work to control the movement of your pelvis. These muscles are often underused in normal activities. As they become more active and toned, you will be increasing your ability to stabilize your upper torso while moving the area below the waist from side to side independently.

Reap the benefits

One of the principal benefits of rotational work is that in stretching and strengthening the oblique muscles you promote the lengthening of the waist area. This reduces pressure on the lower spine and over time helps to create a more streamlined outline to your body. It is advisable to approach these exercises with caution if you have an existing back problem.

HIP ROLLS

Do not be overambitious when you first try this exercise. It looks simple, but it is very deceptive. The measure of "success" is not how far you can drop your knees, but whether you can control the independent movement of your pelvis while maintaining the stability of the upper body. Key points to remember while doing the exercise are: keep your knees and ankles together (visualize them as a single "leg"); keep both shoulders on the floor; and keep your centring muscles engaged throughout the movement.

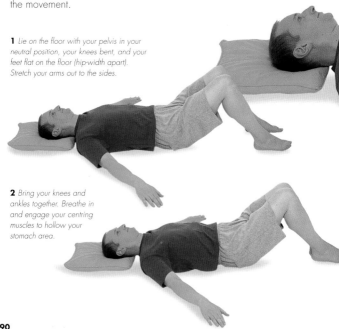

1 Lie on the floor with your pelvis in your neutral position, your knees bent, and your feet flat on the floor (hip-width apart). Stretch your arms out to the sides.

2 Bring your knees and ankles together. Breathe in and engage your centring muscles to hollow your stomach area.

3 As you breathe out, use your abdominal muscles to lift your left hip and tip your knees towards the right. Do not allow your knees and ankles to slide apart. Keep the outer edge of your right foot on the floor and allow your left foot to lift up completely. Keep both shoulders on the floor and stop when you feel your left shoulder beginning to lift.

4 Breathe in and then, on the out-breath, bring your legs back to the centre. Control the entire movement with your centring muscles. Repeat the whole process on the other side. Then complete five repetitions on each side.

Isolating the Pelvis and Legs

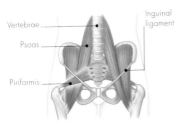

Vertebrae

Psoas

Piriformis

Inguinal ligament

Hip control

A complex arrangement of muscles and ligaments surround the hip joint and control the movement of the legs.

One of the goals that you are aiming for is to stabilize the pelvis in order to encourage and develop maximum freedom of movement of the hip joints and legs. When most people move their legs when walking, for example, they use a lot of movement from the pelvis rather than exploiting the whole potential range of movement of the hip. This tends to pull the pelvis out of alignment and results in stiffness of the hips, because their full range of movement is underused. When you have learned to stabilize your pelvis and increase your hip mobility, you will find that your movements become more economical and you will therefore tire less easily. Your actions will also become more graceful as your body will be much better balanced.

In Pilates you will learn that stability is not the same as rigidity, in which there is tension throughout the body. You will develop the ability to create stillness in one area by engaging, but not tensing, the relevant muscles. This allows you to move and relax nearby areas without restriction. There is no short cut to achieving this ability but, if you practise the exercises regularly, paying attention to every detail of the instructions, you will soon learn to isolate and stabilize different areas of your body. You will also recognize the sensation of engaging your all-important centring muscles without any tension.

Freeing the hips

In the exercises on the following pages you will develop your ability to move your legs independently of your pelvis, both laterally and forward and back. The objective is not to move each leg very far although, with practice, as your muscles and ligaments lengthen, you will probably find that the distance you can move them does increase. The true goal is to achieve the leg movement while keeping your pelvis completely still. Try not to focus on the distance your leg moves – this is the least important part of the exercise.

This technique actually requires concentration (without tension) and body awareness much more than physical strength. You will probably find the technique difficult to begin with, but persevere. The knee drops also have the subsidiary benefit of stretching and lengthening the inner thigh muscles, but this only starts to happen once you have learned to stabilize the pelvis.

KNEE LIFTS AND DROPS

Perform these lifts and drops lying down, with your knees bent and in the neutral pelvis position. Spend a few moments renewing your sense of alignment and focusing on the even distribution of your weight over the balance points of the feet. Check that your neck is relaxed and lengthened and that your shoulders are relaxed away from your neck. Maintain a sense of elongation from neck to tailbone throughout the exercise.

1 Start in the basic alignment position (see pages 48–51) with your knees hip-width apart. Breathe in.

2 As you breathe out allow your right knee to drop slowly down towards the floor. Keep your pelvis and left leg stable throughout this movement, using your centring muscles. Avoid pressing down too hard on your left foot.

3 Bring your knee slowly back to the centre on the in-breath, controlling the movement with your centring muscles. Repeat the whole process on the other side. Complete a total of five repetitions on each side.

Foot relaxed

Stable pelvis

4 Return to the alignment position. Breathe in and on the out-breath raise your right leg, slowly peeling your foot off the floor to a height of about 30 centimetres (12 inches) and keeping the knee at a right angle. Focus the movement in your hip joint and keep your pelvis stable throughout. Return your foot to the floor on the next in-breath. Repeat on the other side. Complete a total of five repetitions on each side.

Freeing the Pelvis

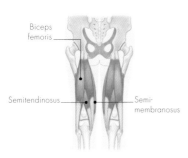

Biceps
femoris

Semitendinosus

Semi-
membranosus

Location of the hamstrings
*The three hamstring muscles
extend from the pelvis down the
back of the thigh.*

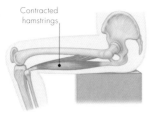

Contracted
hamstrings

Shortened hamstrings
*When the hamstrings remain contracted
for long periods they become
shorter and stiff.*

We have seen how Pilates aims to achieve a balance between strength and stability as well as mobility and freedom of movement. In the exercise on pages 98–99, you will be learning to free the hamstring muscles.

What are the hamstrings?

This group of three muscles runs from the back of the pelvis to the knee and is responsible for bending the knee. The hamstrings can become shortened and inflexible as a result of sitting in chairs. When the knees are bent like this the muscles become lazy, as they are relaxed, but unstretched. The result is that when we try to adopt a position in which they should reach their full length, movement is restricted. This is shown by the difficulty that most Western adults experience when they try to sit on the floor with their legs extended. Shortened hamstrings also tend to pull the pelvis out of alignment, distorting the spine and flattening the lumbar curve.

Be patient

If you have never paid any attention to your hamstrings before, don't expect miracles in a few exercise sessions. These muscles will probably need regular and gentle stretching over several weeks or more. If you try to rush this process by forcing a stretch beyond comfortable limits, you will not only fail to improve more quickly, but you may cause muscle damage that could make you stiffer than when you started. The correct technique for any stretching exercise is to create a gentle, continuous pull. This should not cause any pain and the stretching sensation should gradually ease as you breathe into the position.

Beware of Bouncing

One thing you should never do is to "bounce" the body part in question in an effort to take a stretch further. This has the opposite effect from that intended, as the overstressed muscle fibres actually contract to protect themselves from damage. So take your stretching exercises slowly in order to achieve the maximum progress possible.

Scarf
You can use a scarf just as effectively as a Dynaband for the stretching exercises.

HAMSTRING STRETCHES
The Pilates hamstring stretch is carried out in the supine position, which supports the body during the exercise and allows maximum relaxation. You will need a long scarf or Dynaband to stretch against. Remember that effective stretching should be a relaxing part of your routine. However, this does not mean that you can perform the exercise in a sloppy way; it requires as much precision as any other Pilates movement. Be sure to give an equal stretch to each leg.

1 *Lie down in the alignment position (see pages 48–51). Bend your right knee and wrap the Dynaband under your foot. Take hold of each end of the band with your arms away from your sides. Imagine a straight line from your elbows, through your wrists, and along the length of the Dynaband.*

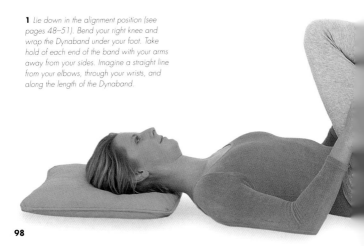

2 *Breathe in. On the out-breath straighten the leg against the resistance of the Dynaband. Lengthen your leg as if stretching your heel towards the ceiling. Take the stretch as far as is comfortable, raising your leg towards the vertical position. Don't lock the knee. Breathe easily through the stretch, keeping your whole body relaxed and your weight evenly supported on your left foot. Repeat on the left side.*

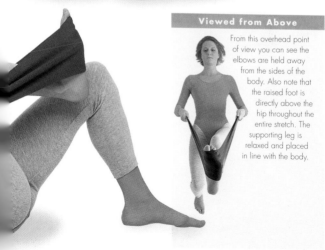

Viewed from Above

From this overhead point of view you can see the elbows are held away from the sides of the body. Also note that the raised foot is directly above the hip throughout the entire stretch. The supporting leg is relaxed and placed in line with the body.

Strengthening the Abdominals

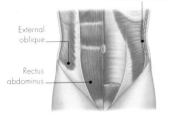

Transversus abdominus

External oblique

Rectus abdominus

The abdominal muscles
These muscles provide support for the entire torso, including the back area.

It will be clear by now that strengthening the abdominals is the key to successful body control. Virtually all Pilates exercises involve the centring muscles, which includes the abdominals, to some extent. There are, however, certain exercises that are aimed specifically at building strength in the abdominal area. The abdominal curls on the following pages should become a key element in your Pilates programme. With regular practice your strength and control will improve.

The muscles

Traditional sit-ups focus on the rectus abdominus muscle, which forms the vertical layer of muscle in the centre of the abdomen, most familiar as the "six-pack" muscle. This muscle helps to curl the head and legs in towards the centre of the body. Pilates curls also engage the transversus muscles that run horizontally from the centre of the abdomen to the spine. The combined action of the muscles has a flattening effect on the abdomen. The abdominal curl also emphasizes the deeper muscles of the abdomen, which provide support and strength to the back.

The abdominal muscles often become ineffective through lack of use. They can also become slack as a result of excessive weight gain or poor posture, both of which stretch and weaken the muscles. In some cases the abdominal muscles seem well developed, but nevertheless fail to provide effective support for the back and abdominal organs. This can be caused by performing abdominal exercises without pulling the navel to the spine. The rectus abdominus then dominates the exercise, bulging outward and preventing the transversus muscles from becoming fully engaged.

Achieving abdominal strength

The abdominal curl demands concentration and attention to detail. Performed correctly it will strengthen and flatten the abdomen. It is very important that you do not attempt to work beyond your strength or you will be unable to maintain the precision of your movements and may strain your back and neck, or start to work the wrong muscles. As long as your stomach is hollowed throughout the curl, your spine will be protected and your rectus and transversus abdominus muscles will be working together correctly. Stop as soon as you are unable to maintain a hollow stomach.

ABDOMINAL CURLS

There are many variations on this exercise so if you attend a Pilates class you may find that your teacher uses a slightly different version than the one shown here. However, there are two elements that all Pilates-style abdominal curls have in common: the emphasis on hollowing the stomach during the entire movement and the need to coordinate the effort with an out-breath. It will help if you visualize the path of the movement of the head as an arc. Remember to work to your own limits.

1 Lie on your back in the alignment position (see pages 50–51). Place both hands behind your head. During the curl use your hands to support the weight of your head, not to force or lead the movement with your neck.

2 Breathe in. As you exhale, engage your pelvic floor, hollow your stomach area, and start to curl your chin towards your chest, leading with the top of your head. Visualize each vertebra peeling off the floor in turn. Keep your chin in a neutral position and make sure your neck and throat are relaxed and your shoulders are down. Direct the movement towards the centre of your body, with your ribs and the muscles in your upper abdomen pulling down towards your navel and your lower abdominals in towards your waist. Keep your pelvic floor engaged.

Release

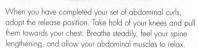

When you have completed your set of abdominal curls, adopt the release position. Take hold of your knees and pull them towards your chest. Breathe steadily, feel your spine lengthening, and allow your abdominal muscles to relax.

3 *When you have curled as far as you can on the out-breath, hold the position and inhale. On the next out-breath slowly uncurl, keeping your stomach hollow and your abdominals in control of the movement. Repeat the whole exercise six times.*

Working on Your Front

Prone position
This is the starting point for most of the exercises carried out on your front.

The next group of exercises involves working on your front in the "prone" position. In this position you become more aware of the air in your lungs expanding the back of the ribcage. You can also focus on the placement of your shoulder blades and accustom yourself to the way they feel when they are correctly positioned down your back. This is also the best position in which to practise back extension exercises. These strengthen the erector spinae muscle that extends down the spine and those that link the backs of the vertebrae.

Body awareness

Before you start exercising in the prone position spend a few moments lying on your front and adjusting your alignment in this position. Here is a checklist of points to look out for:

• Your feet should be parallel with each other, in line with your hips.

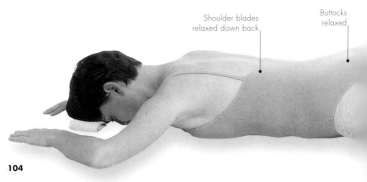

Shoulder blades
relaxed down back

Buttocks
relaxed

- Your pelvis should be level.
- Your buttocks and abdomen should be relaxed.
- Feel the bones of your pelvis sinking into the floor.
- Your ribs should be relaxed downwards into the floor.
- Your shoulder blades must be relaxed down your back.
- Your arms should be relaxed, either at your sides or bent so that your hands are by your head.
- Lengthen your neck in line with your spine.
- Your forehead can rest on your hands or on a thin cushion.

Breathing awareness

When you are aligned lying on your front, practise your breathing.
- Breathe in, expanding the back of your ribcage.
- Breathe out, drawing your ribs and shoulder blades down towards your waist, engaging your lower abdominal muscles and maintaining the stability of your lower back.

If you find it hard to know if your abdominal muscles are engaged in this position, place your hand under your stomach, inside the hip bone, and you should be able to feel your muscles engage and relax.

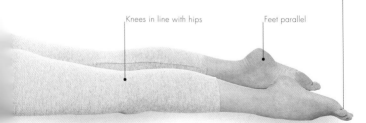

Knees in line with hips

Feet parallel

BACK EXTENSION

The range of movement of the spine is much less bending backwards (extension) than bending forwards (flexion). So do not expect to move very far when you are performing this exercise. The important point to remember is to keep your lower abdomen engaged and stable on the floor, while achieving a sense of lengthening in the neck and upper back. Do not push on your arms – use them mainly for balance. It may take a few tries to get this exercise right, but you will know you have done so when you feel a stretch from your neck to your middle back.

1 *Lie on your front on the floor with your feet parallel, hip-width apart. Place your bent arms at your sides with your hands palms down. Rest your forehead on a thin layer of padding such as a folded towel.*

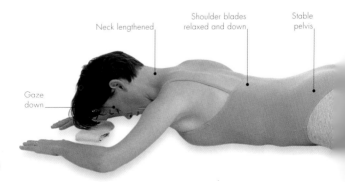

Neck lengthened

Shoulder blades
relaxed and down

Stable
pelvis

Gaze
down

One Step Further

Few of us undertake activities that allow us to incorporate back extension movements into our daily lives and consequently the muscles that govern this action are weak in most people. Therefore be prepared to put in a few weeks of practice with this exercise, in order to build your strength gradually without the risk of strain, before graduating to the more demanding progression of the back extension, the Javelin (see page 182).

2 Breathe in. On the out-breath feel your shoulder blades slide down your back. When you feel a stretch up the back of the neck, lengthen the neck further from the body by lifting the head a little. Keep your gaze turned downward. Return to your starting position on the in-breath. Repeat the whole process six times.

Legs extended and relaxed

Lengthening the Legs from a Stable Centre

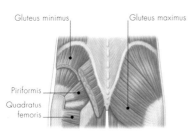

Gluteus minimus

Gluteus maximus

Piriformis

Quadratus femoris

Buttock muscles

The muscles illustrated above are responsible for working the hip joint and are involved in postural alignment.

The prone leg stretch that follows develops stability and strength in the pelvic area and helps to lengthen the spine and legs. It also builds on your ability to work the hips and legs independently of the torso. This is perhaps the most subtle and therefore most difficult aspect of the movement. You will need to engage your full powers of concentration and body awareness to be sure that you are working as intended.

The gluteals

One of the key muscle groups you will be learning to identify and isolate here are the gluteals. These are the buttock muscles, of which the gluteus maximus is the most important. This is the large muscle that extends from the sacrum and coccyx to the upper part of the femur (thigh bone). The gluteals control sideways and backwards movement of the thigh. They are also important for maintaining the position of the pelvis and therefore play a vital part in your posture and alignment.

Although this is a powerful muscle group, the gluteals are also notoriously "lazy". It requires considerable effort and concentration to make them work effectively. This can be achieved only by isolating the muscles from others that normally help initiate the movements in question, including back and abdomen muscles. When you stabilize the pelvis, the gluteals have no choice but to work

Hip mobility

Leg movement originates in the hip joint
(see also pages 92–93). Freedom of
movement relies as much on the mobility
of the joint as on engagement of the
muscles around it. One of the benefits
of the prone leg stretch is that it helps
mobilize the hip joint by stretching the
muscles and ligaments that surround it.

Preparation

Before you start the exercise, spend
some time adjusting your alignment in
the prone position. In particular, pay
attention to the position of your shoulder
blades; make sure that they are relaxed
down your back away from your ears.

Progression

The prone leg stretch is a preparatory exercise
for the diagonal stretch on pages 176–179.
When you are confident that you have
mastered the basic exercise, you will be
ready to move on to the more advanced level.

PRONE LEG STRETCH

This exercise may look simple, but it requires careful co-ordination of stability at the centre and freedom of movement of the hips and legs. Practise the breathing in this position, ensuring that when you engage the centring muscles you are keeping your pelvis in neutral and are not lifting the hips off the floor or tightening the lower back. Try to feel your stomach hollowing in this position.

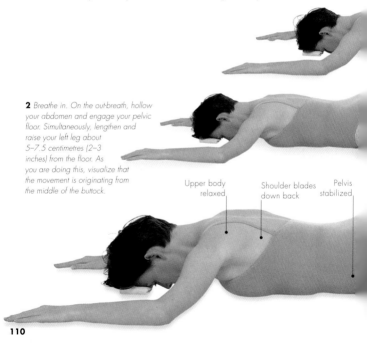

2 Breathe in. On the out-breath, hollow your abdomen and engage your pelvic floor. Simultaneously, lengthen and raise your left leg about 5–7.5 centimetres (2–3 inches) from the floor. As you are doing this, visualize that the movement is originating from the middle of the buttock.

Upper body relaxed

Shoulder blades down back

Pelvis stabilized

1 *Adopt the prone resting position described on page 104. Widen your legs a little and stretch out your arms above your head, keeping your elbows bent. Take a few breaths into your ribs and engage your centring muscles to lift your abdomen towards your spine on each out-breath.*

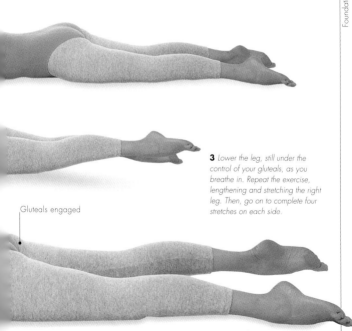

3 *Lower the leg, still under the control of your gluteals, as you breathe in. Repeat the exercise, lengthening and stretching the right leg. Then, go on to complete four stretches on each side.*

Gluteals engaged

Strengthening the Inner Thigh

Isolating the movement

Effort is concentrated in the buttocks and inner thighs, while the upper part of your body is relaxed.

Continuing work with the muscles of the pelvis, buttocks, and thighs, the next exercise, the prone inner thigh squeeze described on pages 114–115, focuses on isolating the inner thigh and the pelvic floor from the gluteal muscles. These muscles are literally the basis for the girdle of strength. When toned and active they contribute to the stability of the entire torso and, in particular, provide a firm anchor for free movement of the legs from the hips. By working the pelvic floor and inner thigh areas separately from the gluteals, you can work the pelvic floor in more depth.

Small but effective

One of the key features of Pilates exercise is that the effectiveness of the movements is in no way dependent on their size. A very tiny change of position, provided that it is carried out with control and precision will, over time, deliver huge benefits in terms of muscle conditioning and overall body appearances. The prone inner thigh squeeze is an excellent example of this. It engages the muscles at the base of the pelvis against the resistance of a small pillow or rolled towel. Through this almost imperceptible movement you will learn what it feels like to use these muscles and understand how to use them under conscious control. Repeated practice of this exercise teaches the body new habits and enables you to

bring these muscles into play – in situations where previously you moved in a way that incurred the risk of strain.

Focus on relaxation

One of the things that many newcomers to Pilates find hard is to relax the areas that are not being worked. It seems more natural to give our conscious control over to making an effort. However, in Pilates the relaxation of key areas during an exercise is as important as the engagement of the muscles in other areas. This is because, in many cases, unwanted tension in a muscle can distort the action of another muscle by subtly altering alignment or resisting the intended movement. In the following exercise it is important to relax the lower legs and feet as well as the upper body and shoulders. As you perform the exercise, constantly recheck your technique to make sure that tension is not creeping into the areas that should be relaxed.

PRONE INNER THIGH SQUEEZE

In this exercise it is important to retain a sense of lengthening from the waist up through the spine and down towards the pelvis. At the same time keep your shoulder blades relaxed down your spine. Use a pillow to support your abdomen if you feel your lower back hollowing during the exercise. Maintain engagement of all your centring muscles, but aim to focus the main effort in the inner thigh area. Do not let muscle tension spread to your lower legs or feet.

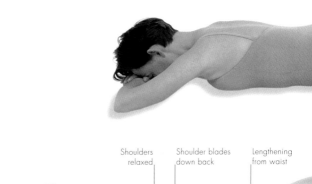

Shoulders
relaxed

Shoulder blades
down back

Lengthening
from waist

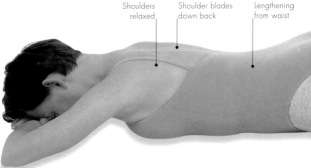

Progression

Along with the back extension exercise on page 106, the prone inner thigh squeeze forms part of the preparation for the Javelin exercise (see page 182). Make sure you can complete this exercise accurately before attempting the more demanding Javelin. Ensure that you feel confident doing the basic exercise before attempting to progress. This will prevent unnecessary strain and possible injury. Remember also to relax before starting an exercise. This has a dual effect: harmonizing your mind and body makes it easier to focus, and the spine lengthens more effectively when the surrounding muscles are relaxed.

1 *Lie on the floor in the prone position with your forehead resting on your hands. Relax your shoulders downwards. Bring your legs together and place a pillow or rolled towel between your upper thighs.*

Engage buttocks and pelvic floor

Squeeze inner thighs

2 *Breathe in. On the out-breath engage your centring muscles and hollow your abdomen to support your lower back. At the same time squeeze the pillow with your inner thigh muscles and then engage your buttock muscles. Keep your feet relaxed and resting on the floor. Relax back to the normal position as you breathe in again. Repeat the whole process ten times.*

Freeing the Fronts of the Thighs

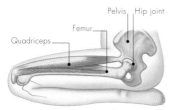

Kneeling stretch

Kneeling can be difficult if your quadriceps muscles are shortened. Regular stretching increases your flexibility.

Pelvis   Hip joint

Femur

Quadriceps

You have already learned to stretch the hamstrings at the back of the thigh (see pages 98–99). However, you also need to stretch the muscles at the front of the thigh. These muscles are known as the quadriceps, or quads. These particular muscles work in opposition to the hamstrings. Contraction of the quadriceps extends the leg, straightens the knee, and lifts up the thigh. Relaxation of these muscles allows the knee to bend fully and permits freedom of movement of the hip joint.

Causes of quad shortening

Both underuse and overtraining can result in stiff and shortened quads. Cycling, in which the quads are under almost constant tension, is an example of a sport that can cause shortening of the quads unless regular counter-balancing stretches are performed. Shortening of the quads may also result from or contribute to postural problems linked to misalignment of the pelvis. The result of shortened quads is reduced flexibility in the knees and stiff movement of the legs.

Choosing your stretch

There are several techniques for stretching the quadriceps. Choose from those that are shown on the following pages to find the one that you feel most comfortable with or alternatively vary your choice of exercise to avoid monotony in your Pilates programme. All quad stretches rely on maintaining

an immobile pelvis to provide a firm
base from which to work the muscles.
As with other stretches, the quad
exercise should provide a gradual
lengthening of the muscle fibres. Never
"bounce" into the stretch in a misguided
attempt to maximize the effect. The
result will be further shortening as the
muscle tenses to protect itself against
further strain. Therefore you should take
the stretch only as far as is comfortable
for you. As you hold the position,
breathe steadily and use your
exhalation to boost the degree of
relaxation and take the stretch a little
further. But don't be overambitious –
stop if you feel any pain at all. Take
special care if you have a tendency to
suffer from knee problems, since most
quad stretches involve bending the
knee. It is often best to seek expert
advice before you embark on such
exercises if you know you have a
history of problems.

QUAD STRETCHES

Three alternative quad stretches are shown here. Don't do them all during a single exercise session; rather choose whichever you feel most comfortable with. If you suffer from knee problems, the standing stretch is most suitable. Hold each stretch for a count of 20, breathing easily and steadily throughout. Try to release tension in your body as you perform the stretch.

Prone quad stretch

Start in the prone position (see page 104). Keep your pelvis stable and "rooted" to the floor throughout. Bring one foot back towards your buttocks. Catch the foot with your hand if you can reach or with a scarf if you can't. Pull your heel slowly and steadily towards the centre of your buttocks. Feel a gentle stretch in the front of the thigh. Repeat on the other side.

Kneeling quad stretch

Kneel with your knees together. Place your hands behind your hips and relax your shoulders. Breathe in and on the out-breath use your centring muscles to tilt your pelvis upward. Feel the stretch in the fronts of the thighs. Repeat five times.

Standing quad stretch

Stand with your feet hip-width apart. Have a chair or other support by your side. Engage your centring muscles and grasp one foot. Keep your pelvis aligned and neutral and your knees together as you bring your heel towards the centre of your buttocks. Maintain a sense of lengthening throughout. Repeat on the other side.

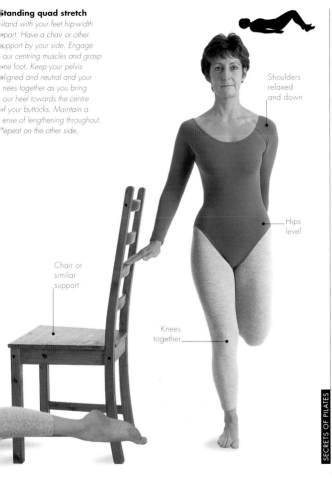

Shoulders relaxed and down

Hips level

Chair or similar support

Knees together

119

Lengthening the Spine

Comfort and relaxation
*If your knees are stiff, support
yourself in the rest position
with cushions as shown.*

In a well-designed Pilates programme
the exercises are selected to balance
both effort and relaxation in each
group of muscles. This important
principle ensures that muscles that have
worked hard do not overshorten as a
result of the effort. A counterbalancing
stretch during your Pilates session will
ensure that the muscles are lengthened
as well as toned to provide maximum
mobility alongside increased strength.

Many of the prone exercises
described on the previous pages
involve the extension of the spine. These
movements can be strenuous and
demanding so the final element of the
prone exercises provides a welcome
and relaxing counterbalance,
incorporating an effective spinal stretch
that flexes the spine and releases any
muscle tension that may be evident in
the muscles that link each of the
individual vertebrae.

Relaxation

It is often difficult to relax if you are
uncomfortable. If you are feeling pain
in any part of your body, this will set up
tension throughout the rest of the body,
preventing the muscles from relaxing
and lengthening. It is therefore
important that you do not experience
any discomfort when performing muscle
releasing exercises.

For the exercise on pages 122–123
there are several ways you can ease
any discomfort you may feel. For
example, your knees may be stiff, so try
placing cushions under your knees and
ankles and/or between your calves
and buttocks. Using such support does
not in any way diminish the value of the
exercise. Experiment to find out which
arrangement works best for you, then
use it after exercising.

While you are in the relaxation position you can practise your rib breathing, which will increase the stretch to the back. As you breathe in, expanding your lower ribs out to the side, imagine that you are trying.to burst out of your T-shirt. Then, on the out-breath, let the ribs release and gently engage the centring muscles.

Completing your relaxation

The way in which you get up from a relaxation position is sometimes as important as how you perform it. After all, there would be little purpose in spending time releasing tense muscles if you misuse them as soon as the exercise session has come to an end.

It is possible to prolong and reinforce the positive effects of the rest position by paying particular attention to how you return to the upright position afterwards. The instructions on the next page include guidance on how to get up after you have completed this exercise. There is also a lying-down variation if you have knee problems.

REST POSITION

Use this position to stretch out the spine after you have worked your back in the prone position. Although it is intended to be relaxing, the position nevertheless requires the engagement of the centring muscles. This action gently flexes the spine, releasing tension in the muscles and ligaments that link the vertebrae. You should feel a satisfying stretch that lengthens the spine from the lumbar area when doing this exercise. Two versions of it are shown here: the classic unsupported position and an alternative stretch lying on the side. The latter position is best for those who have knee problems.

1 Kneel on all fours, knees directly under your hips and hands under your shoulders.

2 Move your buttocks back towards your heels and sink down so that your forehead is on the floor. Keep your hands in their starting position. Breathe in and feel your spine lengthening. Rest in this position for a few breaths.

4 Flex your feet and adopt a squatting position, keeping your centring muscles engaged. Keep your feet parallel, and on an out-breath roll up to a standing position.

3 Get up from the rest position slowly. Breathe in and bring your navel to spine. Uncurl gradually, starting from the base of the spine. Visualize your tailbone moving downwards. Keep your shoulders down and uncurl your head last.

Lying-down Variation

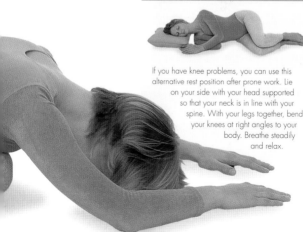

If you have knee problems, you can use this alternative rest position after prone work. Lie on your side with your head supported so that your neck is in line with your spine. With your legs together, bend your knees at right angles to your body. Breathe steadily and relax.

Basic Standing Position

The tripod
Your weight should be evenly distributed through these three balance points on the sole of each foot.

Standing correctly

Correcting your standing posture is perhaps the most important contribution Pilates can make to your daily life. Just because we all spend time standing as part of our normal routine, it doesn't mean that we know how to do it correctly. In fact, most people's standing posture includes a long list of faults. Pilates gradually teaches you how to eliminate these faults, but because habits are deeply ingrained, it will take time and determination to ensure that you always stand correctly.

One of the advantages of standing posture work is that you can practise anytime, anywhere. Think about your posture when you are standing in a supermarket queue or waiting for a bus and try the active standing procedure described on pages 126–127. Nobody else will notice, but you will feel the benefit as you reduce the strain on your back and overcome tiredness. Of course, after regular practice, eventually others will notice the effects because you will look taller and younger, and feel more energetic.

Posture principles

When standing you should be aiming to reproduce in the upright position the alignment you achieved in the exercise on page 50. Working from your feet upwards you should have your:

• weight distributed equally over the balance points on the soles of your feet (see above)
• feet hip-width apart and parallel
• knees soft and facing forwards
• pelvis in your neutral position

centring muscles engaged
shoulder blades relaxed down
our back
shoulders away from your ears
head comfortably balanced directly
ver your spine
chin held slightly in.

till but active

imply standing is not a rest position,
lthough when you do it correctly it can
ndeed be relaxing. To hold your body
pright you need to actively engage
nany different muscles. Inappropriate
ackness of any of the vital support
nuscles can lead to excessive strain
n another group of muscles. For
xample, if your abdominal muscles
re not properly engaged when you
re standing, your back will be forced
o take a greater load. You should
herefore aim to engage opposing
roups of muscles equally, and without
xcessive effort, to create a sense of
alance and lightness throughout your
ody. In effect, your static body is
oised between rest and action.

ACTIVE STANDING

The active standing exercise shown here will help you to achieve balance and alignment. When you practise at home, work in front of a full-length mirror to see how the adjustments you make are affecting your outward appearance. Once you know how it feels to stand in this way, use this position as the starting point for all of the standing exercises that are illustrated in the book and use it to re-establish your sense of equilibrium after doing them, too.

Heel Lifts and Toe Raises

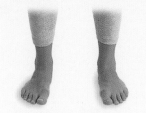

Improve your balance when standing by practising rolling forwards onto the balls of your feet, allowing your heels to lift from the floor, and then rolling back so that your weight concentrates on your heels and your toes lift a little. Engage your centring muscles to stabilize your torso. Use a support for balance, if necessary.

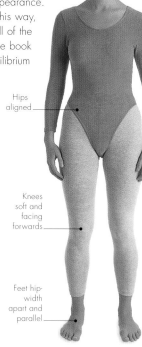

Hips aligned

Knees soft and facing forwards

Feet hip-width apart and parallel

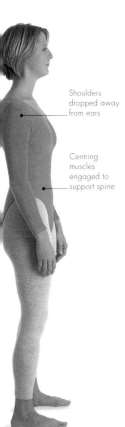

Shoulders dropped away from ears

Centring muscles engaged to support spine

Pelvic Tilts in Standing Position

To find your neutral position practise a few pelvic tilts in a standing position.

Tilt the pubic bone forwards to flatten the lumbar curve.

Tilt the pelvis back to increase the lumbar curve. Then return to a neutral position between the two extremes.

Knee bends

Reinforce your stability and alignment in the standing position by practising knee bends. Breathe in and on the out-breath bend your knees, keeping them in line with your feet. Bend as far as you can without lifting your heels. Breathe in and straighten up. Maintain alignment throughout.

Spine Awareness

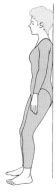

Support and alignment
Using a wall for support promotes alignment and precision in this exercise.

You probably already know that your spine is not a single unit but an articulated column that is made up of 34 different bones. To use and develop your back with sensitivity it is important to keep the idea of this segmented structure at the forefront of your mind. Many exercises in Pilates are based on this understanding of the inherent but limited mobility in the back, which is both freed and supported by engagement of the centring muscles in all movements of the torso.

In your exercise programme you will be developing your ability to maximize the range of movement in the spine, but also to contain that movement within safe parameters. To do this you need to foster your ability to recognize and control the muscles that are the proper initiators of the action. In particular, you need to develop an appreciation of how working the deep abdominal muscles protects and strengthens your back as it flexes and extends.

The roll down is a classic Pilates exercise, a deceptively simple concept that incorporates the need to carry out a carefully co-ordinated sequence of actions. It helps to encourage mobility of the spine, and uses the centring muscles to direct and limit the movement. The muscles at the front and back of the body are used in controlled opposition to each other to create the movement while maintaining alignment. The roll down also promotes good

alance and an awareness of the
istribution of weight through the feet.
our legs also need to be active but
hould not dominate the exercise.

sing a wall support

he foundation version of this exercise
ses a wall for support and to promote
lignment. Practise it in this way until
ou are able to work with accurate
lignment without this guidance. Use
whatever imagery helps you to visualize
he movement as a gradual "unpeeling"
rom the wall (or vertical position),
ertebra by vertebra from the neck to
he base of the spine. The reverse
novement, as you slowly straighten up,
lemands equal physical and mental
ngagement. The end of the exercise
hould not be hurried or skimped.

Progression

When you can perform the wall-supported
exercise confidently and accurately, try it from
a free-standing position. You will need to start
from the active standing position on page
126 and use your centring muscles strongly
hroughout to maintain stability and alignment.

ROLL DOWNS FOUNDATION

Prepare for this exercise by finding a clear section of wall that you can work against. As you place yourself against the wall, check to see if there is any tension in any part of your body, but especially in your back and shoulders. Hold your head and neck aligned over the spine as you begin. Your arms should be allowed to hang without tension by your sides.

1 Stand by the wall, your feet hip-width apart from each other and 30 centimetres (12 inches) away from the wall. Lean your back against the wall and bend your knees a little so that they are in line with your ankles. Check that your pelvis is in its neutral position and your sacrum is in contact with the wall.

2 Breathe in, relaxing your shoulder blades down your back. Then breathe out, and feel your ribs sliding down towards your waist. At the same time allow your head slowly to drop forwards, gradually pulling your spine away from the wall vertebra by vertebra. Allow your arms to follow the movement but keep your knees and pelvis stable.

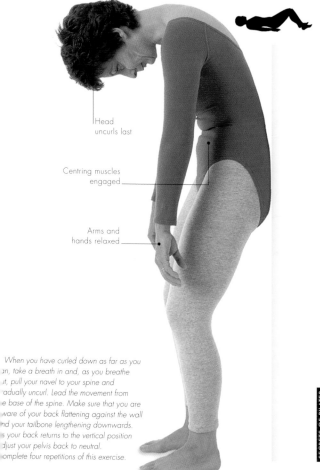

Head
uncurls last

Centring muscles
engaged

Arms and
hands relaxed

When you have curled down as far as you
can, take a breath in and, as you breathe
out, pull your navel to your spine and
gradually uncurl. Lead the movement from
the base of the spine. Make sure that you are
aware of your back flattening against the wall
and your tailbone lengthening downwards.
As your back returns to the vertical position
adjust your pelvis back to neutral.
Complete four repetitions of this exercise.

Groundwork

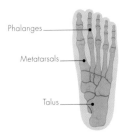

Foot structure

The numerous tiny bones in the foot provide maximum flexibility and strength.

Phalanges

Metatarsals

Talus

Your feet are your point of contact with the ground. They provide stability when you are still and are also the launching point for movement. In philosophical terms they can be seen as your link with the material reality of earth, connecting you to the source from which all living things originate. However, you don't have to take on board such perspectives to realize that the condition of your feet is fundamental to your sense of well-being. Most of us have experienced the huge sense of relief in putting our feet up after a long period of standing or walking. And a good foot massage ca produce a degree of relaxation that may seem disproportionate to the area that is being treated. Not surprisingly, therefore, Pilates gives particular consideration to the feet.

Flexibility

The feet and ankles need to be both strong and flexible to support the weigh of the body and in order to maintain balance. The complex network of bone and joints in the foot distributes the body's weight over the maximum area of the sole. The inherent springiness provided by the arched structure has effective shock-absorbing capabilities as weight is lifted on and off the feet. However, just as with any other part of the body, the efficiency of the feet can be reduced by years of neglect or abuse. Ill-fitting shoes can also distort and cramp the feet and toes and prevent them from spreading out as the receive the body's weight, which is the distributed over a smaller area. Many of us also spend insufficient time walking barefoot. Lack of this fundamental form of foot exercise can lead to reduced muscle tone in the feet.

The Pilates approach

Pilates foot exercises will help you to rediscover flexibility and mobility in your feet and ankles. Rotations of the ankles help to restore their full range of movement. Ankle flexibility permits greater ease of movement through the length of the legs and reduces stress on the back. Repeated flexing and extension of the feet helps maintain muscle tone and the natural flexibility of the foot structure. The feet can work harder for longer without aching and they are able to absorb more of the potentially damaging jarring forces before they are transmitted to the spine. Improved muscle responsiveness also makes it easier to isolate the toes, allowing you to keep them relaxed during exercises when the foot is pointed and to prevent them from curling back when the foot is flexed.

FOOT AND ANKLE EXERCISES

Perform all foot exercises in bare feet. As you rotate your ankles you will need to make a conscious effort to relax. These joints are not used to being idle and tend to tense up as soon as any force – even the gentle force of your hand – is applied. So be patient and give this important mobilization exercise a chance to free your ankles fully. The foot and toe exercises may seem easy until you try them. Most of us are unused to controlling the movement of our toes and the muscles and nerves are often unresponsive to the commands of the brain. The only answer is persistence – you will have to relearn the full potential of your feet gradually.

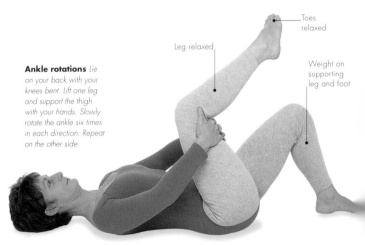

Ankle rotations *Lie on your back with your knees bent. Lift one leg and support the thigh with your hands. Slowly rotate the ankle six times in each direction. Repeat on the other side.*

Toes relaxed

Leg relaxed

Weight on supporting leg and foot

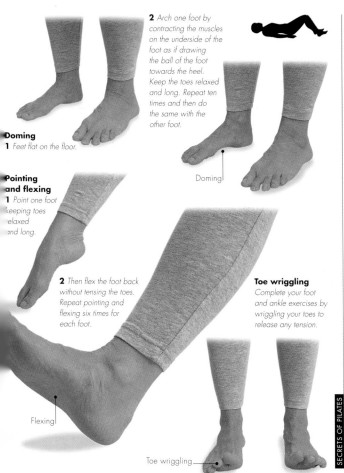

2 Arch one foot by contracting the muscles on the underside of the foot as if drawing the ball of the foot towards the heel. Keep the toes relaxed and long. Repeat ten times and then do the same with the other foot.

Doming
1 Feet flat on the floor.

Doming

Pointing and flexing
1 Point one foot keeping toes relaxed and long.

2 Then flex the foot back without tensing the toes. Repeat pointing and flexing six times for each foot.

Toe wriggling
Complete your foot and ankle exercises by wriggling your toes to release any tension.

Flexing

Toe wriggling

Balancing Through the Feet

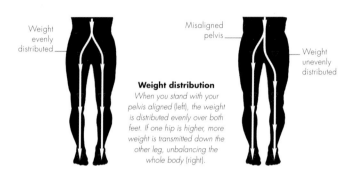

Weight evenly distributed

Misaligned pelvis

Weight unevenly distributed

Weight distribution
When you stand with your pelvis aligned (left), the weight is distributed evenly over both feet. If one hip is higher, more weight is transmitted down the other leg, unbalancing the whole body (right).

The wider the base over which a load is distributed the more stable it is. So when we stand with our feet apart we are less likely to topple over than when standing with our feet close together, or only on one foot. It is also harder to balance a moving load than one that is still; constant shifts are needed to keep the centre of balance over the main load-bearing area. When we are in action, for example when we are walking, our weight is inevitably shifting; constant adjustments are therefore needed in order to keep our weight evenly balanced over our feet. These little adjustments occur unconsciously most of the time because our bodies have acquired the habit of making such movements. But try altering the load, for instance, by carrying a heavy rucksack, and you will become instantly aware of your body having to work to maintain your balance as you walk, stand, and sit. Though your body may unconsciously move to keep you balanced this exercise demonstrates how it can be both stressful on your body and also eventually exhausting.

Minimizing movement

Although your body will have to make adjustments as you move, the Pilates approach to this aspect of body control is to train the body to keep unnecessary movements to a minimum when you are in motion. This reduces the amount of effort that needs to be expended on adjusting and rebalancing after each step. The result is smoother and more graceful actions that are more economical and therefore less tiring.

In the exercises on the following pages you will be practising keeping your body, and in particular your pelvis, stable as you shift your weight from one foot to the other. This teaches you to maintain a level pelvis as you walk, which will minimize effort and reduce strain. The second exercise provides additional practise in keeping your balance through changes in your centre of gravity. It also promotes flexibility of the foot, which is yet another area of the body where the muscles are sadly underused.

PEDALLING

Perform the following exercises barefoot to promote maximum contact between foot and floor and to allow the toes to spread and work most effectively. It is easy to do the pedalling exercise without proper control, so make sure that you focus on the detail of the movement and notice and stabilize any movement in your pelvis. Visualize the joints of your hips, knees, ankles, and feet moving freely, while your pelvis and upper body remain in alignment. Remember to practise the second exercise an equal number of times on each side.

1 *Start in a standing position. Breathe in and feel your spine lengthen. Breathe out and engage the centring muscles. Peel one heel off the floor in a smooth movement as the knee moves forward. Lower the heel and repeat on the other side. Repeat five times.*

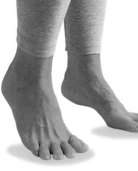

2 *Now practise alternate heel lifts of each foot in a continuous movement, starting to lift the heel on one side as the heel on the other side is lowered.*

3 *Try to achieve a rhythmic pedalling action, keeping your pelvis aligned and stable throughout.*

1 *Start from an active standing position.*

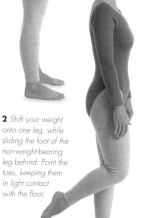

2 *Shift your weight onto one leg, while sliding the foot of the non-weight-bearing leg behind. Point the toes, keeping them in light contact with the floor.*

3 *Breathe in. On the out-breath, keeping your pelvis and torso stable, bend the weight-bearing knee to exert pressure on the toes of the other foot. Pause for a second and return to your starting position. Repeat five times on each side.*

Self-assessment

Developing confidence

As you progress with Pilates, you will gain an increasing sense of fulfilment from the exercises.

If you have practised all the exercises for a few weeks, you may find that you are impatient to undertake some new challenges. To help you decide whether you are ready to move on, it's a good idea to review your progress.

Breathing

By now, you should be finding it much easier to expand and contract your ribcage with each inhalation and exhalation. You should also be finding it more natural to co-ordinate your breathing with the exercises. If you are still finding any aspect of the breathing difficult you should carry on practising at foundation level.

Centring muscles

Awareness of the centring muscles and the ability to engage them on an out-breath to hollow the abdomen is fundamental to the Pilates technique. Nearly all of the basic exercises demand some degree of utilization of these muscles, and by now you should be very familiar with the sensation of the abdomen contracting and supporting your torso. If your control of these muscles is still unreliable – for example, if your tummy still "domes" when you do the abdominal curl – then you are not ready to advance to the more difficult exercises.

Body awareness

Your body awareness will be increasing and it should now be second nature to adjust your pelvis to neutral before starting any exercise. You should be aware of the position of your shoulders and shoulder blades, too. If you still find it hard to feel when your alignment is incorrect, you may need to spend longer on the foundation exercises.

Pain or discomfort

No Pilates exercise should ever cause you any pain. If this occurs you may have an underlying problem or your technique may be wrong. In any case stop exercising and seek professional advice. Do not progress to the next stage. However, a degree of stiffness is normal, particularly the day after a strenuous Pilates workout – it is generally a sign that you have reached muscles that were previously underused. As you become more accustomed to the exercises this will become less noticeable. Freedom from stiffness following exercises that previously caused it is an indicator that you are ready to progress.

Feeling Good

Whether or not you are ready to progress to a more challenging level, you will almost certainly be feeling the benefits of your Pilates practice. Your body will be feeling longer and lighter, and everyday actions will require less effort. This is your main incentive to continue your practice at whatever level suits you.

PROGRESSION
EXERCISES

In this chapter you will be introduced to some exercises of a higher level. These require greater control over your breathing and include more complex combinations of movements. Many of them also rely on a basic level of strength in the centring muscles. Integrate these exercises gradually into your regular routine when you feel you are ready to progress further. ✎ Remember that your Pilates training is not a race, and there is no glory in attempting exercises that you are not ready for. It is better to spend more time than you need on the foundation work than to attempt to progress faster than your body is ready for and run the risk of injury.

Progressing your Breathing

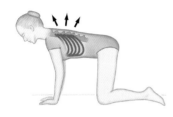

Breathing into the back

In the all-fours position you can develop your awareness of the expansion of the back of the ribcage during inhalation.

Breathing control should always remain the lynchpin of your exercise technique. You will by now have an insight into how the way you breathe affects your whole body, both at rest and during physical effort. You will also be finding it easier to switch to rib breathing as you perform your exercises. Your control of your inhalation and exhalation will have improved considerably and you will also notice that you can expand your

ribcage further with the in-breath and contract it more effectively with the out-breath than when you first started.

While Pilates does not improve heart and lung capacity in the same way as aerobic exercise does, you will notice that you are able to control your breathing more effectively. It will be deeper, so the supply of oxygen to your body will be improved, and the expulsion of waste gases more efficient. This results in more energy and stamina.

Breathing each day

It is easy to build breathing practice into your everyday activities. For example, you can do a few minutes of rib breathing while you are waiting in a queue or sitting at your desk during a break. As you progress with your Pilates programme you will probably find yourself using Pilates breathing techniques naturally to help you use your body more effectively as you exert

effort, such as when lifting or turning.
You will also find that your movements
become more confident and deliberate,
which will reduce the risk of injuries
caused by uncontrolled actions.

Progression exercises

The four-square breathing exercise
on the following pages is designed to
improve your awareness of the action
of the back of the ribcage during
inhalation and exhalation. At the same
time you will be using your centring
muscles to stabilize the curves of your
back. Awareness of the position of the
shoulder blades also forms an important
element of this exercise.

Insights from Alexander

Many of the breathing techniques taught as
part of the Pilates method have much in
common with those used in the Alexander
Technique. This bodywork system is extremely
compatible with Pilates exercises and many
people benefit from learning both methods.

FOUR-SQUARE BREATHING

For this exercise you should position yourself on all fours. Take the time to make sure that your limbs are placed in proper alignment before starting the exercise. The overall objective is to keep the lower part of the body stable while maximizing the expansion of the ribcage into the back. This requires you to engage the centring muscles, including those of the pelvic floor, without creating tension in the upper back or shoulders. The neck needs to be held in line with the spine to avoid increasing the lumbar curve of the back.

1 Kneel on all fours with your hands under your shoulders and your knees under your hips, hip-width apart.

2 Allow your back to hollow down.

3 Now arch your spine, allowing your head to drop down naturally.

4 Return your back to a "neutral" position between hollowed and arched. This is your starting position.

No tension in upper body

Neck relaxed in line with spine

Pelvis stable

5 Engage your centring muscles and breathe into your ribs, concentrating on the expansion of the ribcage into your back. Then breathe out, drawing your ribcage downwards and inwards. Repeat ten times.

147

Enhanced Spine Control

Spine-lift basics

Before performing any spine lift, check that your starting position is aligned and your spine and pelvis are neutral.

By practising the spine lift on pages 86–87, you will have been developing your awareness of the segmented structure of the spine. When you first attempted the spine lift you were perhaps hardly conscious of the separate movement of each vertebra. But as you practised the exercise and increased the mobility of your spine, and by listening to your body, you will have begun to appreciate and be sensitive to the capabilities and limitations of your spine. Your ability to stabilize your torso by engaging your centring muscles will also have increased and you will be able to complete the whole exercise with assurance and ease.

The more challenging exercises on the following pages enable you to take control of your spine one stage further but do not attempt them until you are completely confident and at ease with the basic exercise.

The main challenge of the progressed spine-lift exercises consists of maintaining the stability of the pelvis and not arching the upper back as you raise your arms. The inclusion of movement of the arms in the progressed exercises increases the stretch for the spine and improves your shoulder mobility. It is important to let the curling motion of the spine be controlled by the centring muscles, leaving the shoulders lengthened and relaxed.

The increased complexity of these exercises demands better co-ordination of both movement and breathing and will therefore also benefit the overall fluidity of your actions.

Don't be alarmed if you find the exercises difficult to begin with – they are much more advanced than the basic exercises so you will need to work on them gradually (see box). You will find as you practise them you will be able to lift a little higher each time.

Don't forget your feet

Spine lifts are achieved through a combination of the engagement of the abdominal muscles and pressure that is applied through the feet. As you do the exercises you need to support the overall movement by keeping your weight evenly distributed over the tripod of the feet (see pages 124–127 to remind yourself how to do this). Try to keep your legs and feet stable but relaxed throughout the exercises on pages 150–151.

Advancing Step by Step

Approach all new exercises with care. Your previous Pilates practice will have prepared you to some extent for the new movements but they will also involve different challenges. Don't rush into the most advanced version of a staged exercise; take the time to practise the preparatory steps before attempting the full movement. In this way you will avoid strain and maintain steady progress.

PROGRESSED SPINE LIFT

Two exercises are shown here, both of which are extensions of the foundation spine lift on pages 86–87. Do not progress to these exercises until you are able to perform the basic exercise with full control of the movement using the centring muscles. In both exercises use your abdominals, which should be pulled securely from navel to spine, to lift and then lower the spine vertebra by vertebra. In the overhead stretch version, the arm lift at the end of the spine lift adds a further spine-lengthening quality to the exercise. The feet-to-wall lift demands more abdominal control than the other forms of spine lift. In both of them, lift only as far as you are able to control.

Spine lift with overhead stretch

Make the basic spine lift more challenging by raising your arms overhead on the in-breath then keeping them there as you roll your spine back onto the floor and into a neutral position.

1

2

3

Spine lift with feet to wall

Lie with your feet, hip-width apart, flat against a wall so that your knees are at right angles. Keep your spine lengthened and avoid curling your tailbone.

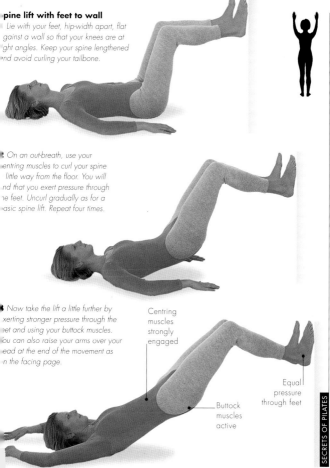

On an out-breath, use your centring muscles to curl your spine a little way from the floor. You will find that you exert pressure through the feet. Uncurl gradually as for a basic spine lift. Repeat four times.

Now take the lift a little further by exerting stronger pressure through the feet and using your buttock muscles. You can also raise your arms over your head at the end of the movement as in the facing page.

Centring muscles strongly engaged

Equal pressure through feet

Buttock muscles active

Pelvic Stability

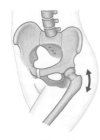

Stable pelvis

With a stable pelvis, movement of the legs is focused in the hip joint, promoting graceful and economic action.

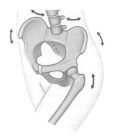

Unstable pelvis

When the pelvis moves as well as your legs, the movement causes stress on the torso and spine.

In Pilates free and effective movement is based on a combination of mobility and stability. Unrestricted movement in a joint is encouraged and developed by stabilizing the area of the body in which it is sited. If the surrounding area moves as well, it "takes over" the movement and the joint does not need to work through its full range. This soon leads to loss of mobility and stiffness. In addition, the inappropriate movement of the part of the body that is supposed to be anchoring the joint creates imbalances and strains elsewhere.

The hip joints, which allow for movement of the legs, work through their full potential only when the pelvis is stabilized by using the centring muscles.

Progressing from the knee lift

The double knee lift and roll described on the following pages is a progression from the knee lift that you learned in the foundation exercises on pages 94–95. Move on to this new exercise when you can perform the foundation exercise easily while maintaining a reliably stable pelvis.

To perform the exercise properly you need to be able to use your centring muscles to control the sideways movement of the pelvis and legs together. The weight of the legs increases the intensity of the exercise. The oblique muscles of the lower abdomen feature strongly in this action. The exercise also relies on the correct use of your breathing to help hollow the abdomen so that the internal abdominal muscles are utilized.

Leading from the hip

The rolling movement in this exercise should originate from the hips, not from the knees. It will help if you visualize your pelvis and both legs as a single unit set in concrete. The spine rotates to allow the pelvis and legs to roll to one side under the control of the centring muscles. The movement continues until the shoulder blade on the other side begins to lift off the floor. When this occurs your centring muscles are no longer in control and you should bring the legs back to the centre.

DOUBLE KNEE LIFT AND ROLL

In the first part of this exercise you need to focus on effectively engaging the centring muscles as well as on using your out-breath to bring your navel towards your spine, hollowing your stomach. In this position your pelvis is quite stable. Do not start to roll your hips until you are sure that you have achieved this. Remember that the measure of your mastery of this exercise is not how far you can roll to the side, but how far you can roll while maintaining pelvic stability. The distance you can roll will increase with practice, but will only occur as the result of improved muscle control.

1 *Lie down with your knees bent in a neutral position. Spread your arms out to the sides. Keeping your centring muscles engaged, on an out-breath raise one knee so that it is above the hip.*

2 On the next out-breath, raise your other knee and position it alongside the first so that they are lightly touching. The knees need to stay together throughout the rest of the movement.

Knees and ankles together

3 Breathe in and on the out-breath roll from the hips towards one side. As you do so turn your head in the opposite direction. Lead the movement with the upper hip and do not let your knees slide apart. When you have rolled as far as you can without the shoulder lifting, return to centre on an out-breath. Repeat five times on each side.

Centring muscles control movement at all times

Shoulders in contact with floor

Easy Sitting

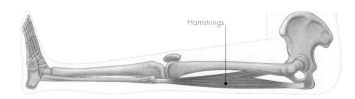

Hamstrings

Y ou may be surprised to discover that sitting, which is such a normal activity, is a progression exercise. However, bodywork specialists from many different disciplines recognize that people living a Westernized lifestyle, which involves long periods spent sitting in chairs, often have great difficulty in sitting on the floor in a strain-free position.

Small children spend much of their time on the floor – crawling, squatting, and sitting in a variety of positions. Their joints are flexible and their key muscles have not shortened as a result of years of unbalanced activity. Sitting on the floor is natural and beneficial to them, but it is a skill that many of us, as adults, have to relearn.

Extending the legs

To sit comfortably with your legs extended you need well-stretched hamstrings.

Problem areas

The main restriction that stops us from sitting (easily) on the floor with our legs extended comes from shortened hamstrings due to lack of use (see also pages 96–99). When these muscles are tight, it is hard to extend the legs and at the same time maintain a straight back when seated. This is because the shortened hamstrings tend to pull the pelvis out of alignment. It also requires very strong centring muscles in order to be able to maintain the spine in an upright position against the pull of shortened hamstrings.

Appropriate exercises

You should already have been
stretching your hamstrings as part of
your foundation routine for at least two
weeks. These stretches continue to be
valuable so you should keep them as
part of your regular programme.

The next step is to try sitting on the
floor with your legs extended out in front
of you, feet parallel but slightly apart.
Focus on distributing your weight evenly
over your sitting bones (you should be
able to feel these bones under your
buttocks when you are sitting down).
Engage your centring muscles to lift your
back into alignment. Unless your
hamstrings are very flexible, you will
probably find that it is difficult to keep
your legs straight out in front of you in
this position. In this case use a firm
cushion to raise your buttocks and
another under your knees for support
when you first start to practise the
exercises illustrated on the following
pages. It may also be helpful to position
yourself with your tailbone flat against a
wall for added support.

SEATED HAMSTRING STRETCHES

The first part of these exercises involves a seated stretch. It is harder work than it looks and needs to be done with careful attention to your technique to ensure that you achieve the necessary stretch. Spend at least a week practising this stretch before moving on to the combined hamstring and back stretch. These extension exercises encourage spinal mobility and back lengthening. Again, it is the precision with which you perform the exercise, rather than the degree of movement you achieve, that will produce positive results.

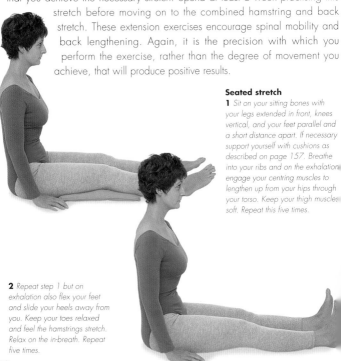

Seated stretch

1 *Sit on your sitting bones with your legs extended in front, knees vertical, and your feet parallel and a short distance apart. If necessary support yourself with cushions as described on page 157. Breathe into your ribs and on the exhalation engage your centring muscles to lengthen up from your hips through your torso. Keep your thigh muscles soft. Repeat this five times.*

2 *Repeat step 1 but on exhalation also flex your feet and slide your heels away from you. Keep your toes relaxed and feel the hamstrings stretch. Relax on the in-breath. Repeat five times.*

ombined hamstring and back stretch

*tting as for the seated stretch, breathe into the
as and on the out-breath allow the weight of the
ad to round the body forward, visualizing
inging your nose towards your navel. Allow
ur back to round but use your centring muscles
maintain a sense of lengthening. Allow your
ms to come forward with the movement. Keep
ur shoulders down and your thighs soft. Roll
ward as far as is comfortable without
llapsing at the centre.*

Hip Rotation

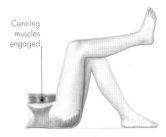

Centring muscles engaged

Stabilizing the centre

Keeping your abdominal muscles engaged in order to stabilize your pelvis is a key aspect of this exercise.

Several exercises in this book focus on the importance of developing pelvic stability alongside the ability to move the legs independently of the pelvis. This will allow you to engage the correct muscles for the job, rather than overworking unnecessary ones. Each exercise furthers your control of this through different types of movement. While having a similar underlying purpose, the varied actions that are incorporated into each of these exercises mobilize, stretch, and engage different groups of muscles.

The area worked

The exercises on the following pages work the deep muscles of the buttocks. Strengthening these muscles provides much more effective and stress-free movement of the hips and legs. In the long term this may reduce wear and tear on the hip joints, which will thereby help to lower the risk of osteoarthritis in later life. Combined with this strengthening action, the hip rotations gently stretch the ligaments that surround and support the joint. This gradually increases the range of movement of the hip joint and therefore also of the leg.

Feeling the stretch

Hip rotations provide a challenge for the centring muscles, as maintaining immobility of the pelvis is of paramount importance. The pelvis needs to be anchored firmly in the neutral position throughout the exercise. In addition, you are also likely to become aware of the work that is undertaken by the deep buttock muscles surrounding the hip. This may be felt at the time as a dull ache around the joint, and on the first occasion you try this exercise may cause stiffness the following day. When you feel this sensation you know that you have reached some of the "forgotten" muscles that the Pilates method identifies as being crucial to effective body use.

Isolating the movement

The ability to engage specific muscles to produce a certain movement while relaxing others nearby is a fundamental Pilates skill. In this exercise it is important to remember to keep your toes softly pointed, but not tense. If the toes are "locked", muscle tension is likely to spread up your leg, restricting and distorting the desired movement.

Turning out

Pilates exercise emphasizes movements that promote outward-turning of the legs from the hip joints. This is because most of us tend to turn in too much – for example, when crossing our legs in a sitting position.

TURNED-OUT KNEE RAISES

This exercise is performed lying on your back. Because of the importance of maintaining a neutral pelvis throughout the movement, it may be advisable to perform a few pelvic tilts, as described on pages 50–51, to establish your neutral position before you start. Your arms remain relaxed throughout the exercise, but you may find it helpful to rest your hands on your lower abdomen to enhance your sense of the stability of the pelvic area.

1 *Lie comfortably in the alignment position (see pages 50–51).*

2 *Breathe out and, with centring muscles engaged, raise one knee. Softly point the toes. Breathe in.*

Softly pointed toes

Stable pelvis

Rotation from hip

3 *Breathe out as you rotate the raised leg within the hip joint, bringing the foot towards the other knee. On an out-breath, return to centre and repeat a further five times. Do the same number of repetitions on the other side.*

Further Abdominal Development

Curl with lifted arms

Bringing your arms back from over your head during the abdominal curl is one way of increasing the challenge.

Curl with arms and legs lifted

Increase the demands on your strength further by lifting both arms and legs during the curl.

Abdominal strength is a core Pilates goal. And one of the key groups of exercises that you need to master in order to achieve that goal is the abdominal curl. In the foundation exercises you will have learned the basic abdominal curl with both hands supporting your head. Do not attempt the exercises on pages 166–167 if you are still finding the foundation version hard: for example, if you have difficulty in supporting the movement with your abdominals. Most people need several weeks' practice before they are ready to progress the abdominal curl.

Increasing the challenge

There are a number of ways in which you can increase the challenge of the abdominal curl. The first is to lengthen the area that is lifted during the exercise. It requires more effort to lift the shoulders from the floor when the arms are extended than when they are held next to the head. The first exercise on the following page incorporates an overhead arm stretch with the abdominal curl. This requires careful co-ordination with your breathing, but once mastered produces a graceful and satisfying movement.

You can also increase the abdominal workload by lifting your legs. In this position, the feet no longer provide a point of leverage for the movement, so the effort is concentrated in the centring muscles. The second progression exercise, which incorporates a knee lift, requires concentration and body awareness to be both effective and safe. The movement must be controlled through your abdominals and not forced by straining the neck forward or arching the spine. If you find this exercise too hard, work on the easier abdominal curls for a bit longer.

The final exercise, the combined curl, is a composite of both movements. It provides a really effective challenge for the abdominals.

Don't Forget to Release

Whichever version of the abdominal curl you choose, always end your practice with the release position described on page 103.

PROGRESSED ABDOMINAL CURLS

Before you start these progressed versions of the abdominal curl, check that your pelvis is securely in neutral. You will need to maintain this position for the first exercise. In the second and third exercises, the lumbar curve inevitably flattens against the floor. However, you need to maintain a sense of the base of your spine lengthening away from the body. Whichever version you are doing, try to retain a sense of the spine stretching as well as curling. Use your engaged centring muscles to prevent yourself from "collapsing" in the middle. Remember to stop if your abdomen starts to bulge or the muscles begin to quiver. This means the exercise is too demanding for you and is a sign that you need to lift less far or revert to an easier version.

Abdominal curl with lifted arms

1 Lie in the alignment position (see page 50) with your arms over your head.

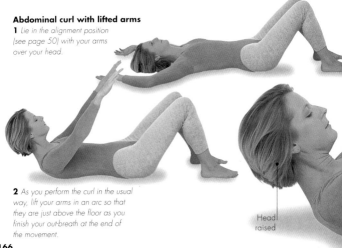

2 As you perform the curl in the usual way, lift your arms in an arc so that they are just above the floor as you finish your out-breath at the end of the movement.

Head raised

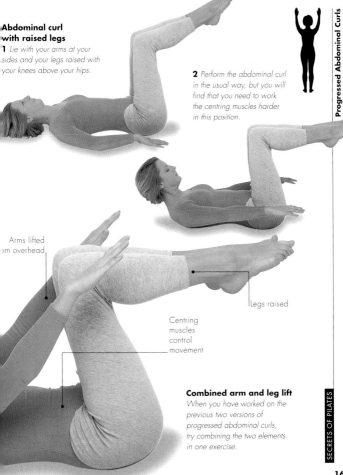

Abdominal curl with raised legs

1 Lie with your arms at your sides and your legs raised with your knees above your hips.

2 Perform the abdominal curl in the usual way, but you will find that you need to work the centring muscles harder in this position.

Arms lifted from overhead

Legs raised

Centring muscles control movement

Combined arm and leg lift

When you have worked on the previous two versions of progressed abdominal curls, try combining the two elements in one exercise.

Understanding the Hundred

A classic Pilates exercise
*The Hundred combines strength,
control, and co-ordination in
a single exercise.*

Perhaps the best known of all the
Pilates exercises, the Hundred finds
a place in almost every Pilates-
based programme. In its original form,
as devised by Joseph Pilates, it
comprises a demanding sequence of
movements that challenges your breath
control, your abdominal strength, and
your overall sense of co-ordination and
body awareness.

Practice and progress

It takes months of practice to be able to
perform the movement in its unmodified
form without strain. However, don't be

discouraged – you can make a start by
practising some of the modified versions
that will gradually build your strength
and co-ordination until you reach the
point where it is possible for you to
complete the full exercise.

The essence of the Hundred

The Hundred is an exercise that relies
on the strength of the centring muscles
being able to support the weight of the
upper body and legs while maintaining
the neutral alignment of the spine.
Pilates himself performed this exercise
with the legs extended and horizontal.
But only the most highly trained Pilates
practitioners are able to prevent their
spine from arching in this position and it
certainly should not be attempted by
beginners. The higher you hold your
legs the less the demands are on your
abdominal strength. Therefore, as a
beginner, you will need to start with
your knees bent. Even when you are
more experienced and are able to work

with straightened legs, do not let them drop lower than an angle of about 45 degrees to the floor.

The name of this exercise derives from the number of repetitions that Pilates recommended. Again this is a final goal to aim for. But, as with all goals, you can't expect to achieve it straight away. Aim to build up from 20 to 30 repetitions, which you can perform in groups with a short rest between. Always aim to build on what you have done before then practise until you achieve the whole Hundred.

Breath control

Breath control is not an optional extra, but an integral part of the exercise. Do not increase the number of repetitions beyond the number for which you can control your breathing. With rhythmic, co-ordinated breathing, the Hundred adds an aerobic element to your Pilates practice and becomes a welcome energizing addition to your programme.

PRACTISING THE HUNDRED

On this page several leg positions are shown for the Hundred, from the recommended starter version, to some variations that allow more intense work. The breathing and arm movements remain the same whichever leg position you choose. Keep reminding yourself that total control of your body alignment is the aim. This can only be achieved with practice over time. After completing the exercise adopt the release position (see page 103).

Beginner's position

From the alignment position (see pages 50–51), on an out-breath, engage the centring muscles and lift your shoulders as for an abdominal curl (see pages 102–103) with your arms stretched forward a little way off the floor. Breathe in for a count of five, beating your arms up and down in a small movement as you do so. Breathe out for a count of five, beating your arms as for the in-breath. Newcomers to this exercise should aim to complete four to six repeats of this exercise (20–30 beats) without a break, building up to ten repeats (100 beats).

Lengthened neck

Flat back

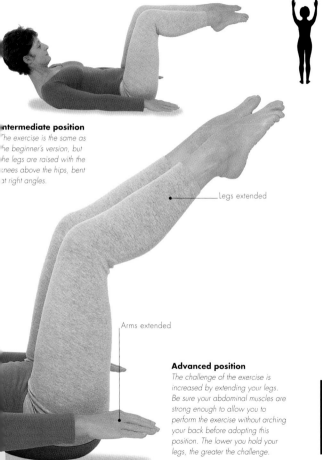

Intermediate position
The exercise is the same as the beginner's version, but the legs are raised with the knees above the hips, bent at right angles.

Legs extended

Arms extended

Advanced position
The challenge of the exercise is increased by extending your legs. Be sure your abdominal muscles are strong enough to allow you to perform the exercise without arching your back before adopting this position. The lower you hold your legs, the greater the challenge.

Working the Obliques

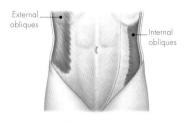

External obliques

Internal obliques

Oblique layers
*The oblique abdominals form the outer
two layers of abdominal muscles
overlying the transverse muscle layer.*

The oblique muscles of the
abdomen run diagonally around
each side to the mid-line of the
abdomen. They are involved in all
twisting movements of the torso and are
also important for stability of the spine,
abdomen, and pelvic area. Well-toned
obliques contribute to the development
of a slim waist and healthy posture.

Abdominals

You need a basic level of abdominal
strength to be able to perform the
diagonal shoulder raise that is illustrated
on the following pages. Don't progress
to working the obliques in this way
until you have been practising the
abdominal curls on pages 102–103
for at least two weeks. The combination
of lifting and twisting involved in these
exercises can easily cause strain if
you have not yet acquired sufficient
abdominal strength to control and direct
the movement safely.

Tips for working the obliques

In the diagonal shoulder raise exercise
(see pages 174–175) the obliques are
used to help raise and turn the torso as
you lift one shoulder up and, at the
same time, twist towards the opposite
hip. The challenge here is not how far
you can lift, but how effectively you can
perform the movement while keeping
your belly hollowed and your pelvis
stable. Keep in mind the following
guidelines:

• Initiate the movement from your
centre, not your neck.

• Aim your armpit, not your elbow,
towards the opposite hip.

- Don't pull the back of your head
forward with your hands.
- Keep your elbows wide and your
chest open throughout the movement.
- Keep your knees and feet hip-width
apart and parallel. If your knees tend to
drift apart during the exercise, grip a
pillow or a rolled-up towel between
them the next time you try it.

Preparation

Develop your sense of this movement by
practising rolling to each side with your
hands behind your head and the lower
elbow resting on the floor.

Sporting twists

Increasing the strength of your obliques
and enhancing the way you use them
in conjunction with the rest of your
abdominal muscles can improve your
overall sports performance and can
help to prevent strain and injury.
Sporting activities that particularly
engage the obliques include golf,
tennis, and squash, all of which involve
twisting movements of the torso.

DIAGONAL SHOULDER RAISE

The diagonal shoulder raise is an exercise that is seen in different forms in many exercise programmes. The key to doing the exercise the Pilates way is to focus on hollowing the belly throughout the lift. If your stomach begins to dome during the exercise it is a sign that you have moved beyond the point where you can control the movement. When this happens you are no longer engaging the muscles correctly and there is no value in lifting any further. You should breathe in and relax down before starting your next repetition.

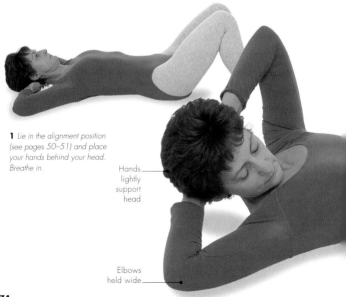

1 Lie in the alignment position (see pages 50–51) and place your hands behind your head. Breathe in.

Hands lightly support head

Elbows held wide

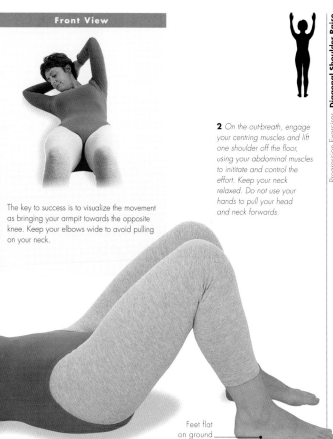

2 On the out-breath, engage your centring muscles and lift one shoulder off the floor, using your abdominal muscles to initiate and control the effort. Keep your neck relaxed. Do not use your hands to pull your head and neck forwards.

The key to success is to visualize the movement as bringing your armpit towards the opposite knee. Keep your elbows wide to avoid pulling on your neck.

Feet flat on ground

175

Towards the Diagonal Stretch

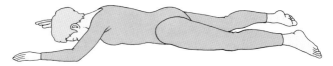

Feeling the stretch

This exercise creates a satisfying stretch up and down the spine from the waist.

The diagonal stretch is a progression from the prone leg stretch that is shown on pages 110–111. The movements involved seem minimal, yet again, but as soon as you try them you will appreciate that they are much harder than you might think at first.

The diagonal stretch strengthens the entire torso. It incorporates work on the shoulder area, stabilizing the structures that support the shoulder joint, which is known as the shoulder girdle. By anchoring this area, the diagonal stretch helps to free the shoulder joint to allow full movement of the arms.

The muscles along the entire length of the spine are then engaged. This back extension work avoids the risk of strain because it is fully supported by the abdominal muscles, which are also engaged throughout the exercise. In the lower part of the torso, stability of the pelvis allows the hip joint to be safely stretched as you extend each leg in turn.

Building up gradually

You are ready to progress to this exercise when you feel confident that you can perform the prone leg stretch with ease. That basic exercise will have taught you how to hollow your abdomen while in the prone position and extend each leg in turn while you are doing so.

The next stage is to learn to extend your arms in the prone position, keeping the same hollowing of the abdomen. Be aware of the centring muscles and be vigilant about the position of your shoulders and shoulder blades, which must still be drawn away from the neck. Although you will be extending the arms, they should remain free from tension at all times. The lengthening effect comes from extending the shoulders, not from straightening the arm by muscle action.

When you have mastered arm extension work, try combining the leg and arm extensions in the full diagonal stretch. Here are some key body awareness pointers for this exercise:
• Be aware of your body lengthening from toe to fingertip.
• Feel the stretch originating from the waist and extending up the spine and down through the sacrum.

Keep your forehead resting on the floor so your neck is relaxed.

DIAGONAL STRETCH VARIATIONS

The diagonal stretch is one of the most demanding but also most satisfying exercises. Performed sloppily it will deliver no benefits, but carried out with focused energy and concentration, you will feel your spine lengthening and strengthening with each repetition. Do not rush to complete the full exercise. Practise the various elements individually to prepare your body for the greater challenge of the combined arm and leg extension.

1 *Lie in the prone position, with your forehead on the floor and your arms extended above your head, and complete a few repetitions of the prone leg stretch on each side (see page 110).*

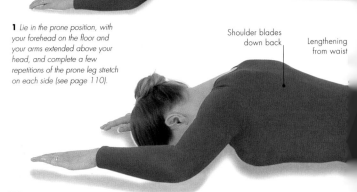

Shoulder blades down back

Lengthening from waist

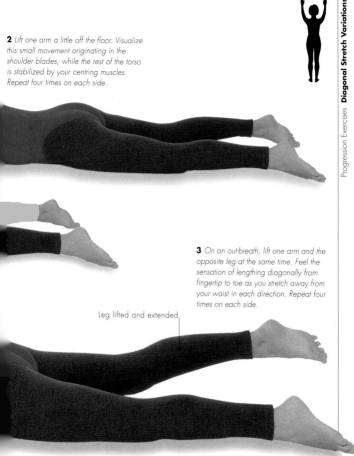

2 Lift one arm a little off the floor. Visualize this small movement originating in the shoulder blades, while the rest of the torso is stabilized by your centring muscles. Repeat four times on each side.

3 On an out-breath, lift one arm and the opposite leg at the same time. Feel the sensation of lengthing diagonally from fingertip to toe as you stretch away from your waist in each direction. Repeat four times on each side.

Leg lifted and extended

The Javelin

Streamlined outline

In this exercise you aim to lengthen your entire body by stretching forward through the spine.

In this exercise, sometimes known as the Arrow, you will be combining the control learned in the prone inner thigh squeeze (see page 114) and the back extension (see page 106). You will need a pillow or rolled towel to place between your thighs and an extra pillow to support your abdomen if necessary. You will also need a layer of padding for your forehead.

Visualizing the shape

As its names suggest, this is a lengthening exercise. As you do this exercise, it is helpful to keep in the forefront of your mind an image of your body acquiring the narrow, streamlined shape of a javelin, spear, or arrow.

Often such visualizations are more effective in directing your body to adopt the required position than a series of dry instructions can be.

It is not only the shape of the body that can be helped by visualization. You can also direct the way that you use your muscles by creating a mental image of the direction of the movement you want to achieve.

Even in a relatively static exercise such as this, you will be initiating the movement of energy in a certain direction. In this case, the head should be visualized as moving forward, but your main energy should be directed through your body from the neck, along the spine and arms, down towards the toes. You should also continue to focus your attention on your breathing in order to ensure that it remains slow and deep throughout the exercise.

Isolating the effort

A key Pilates skill in this exercise is isolation. The muscles of the abdomen, pelvic floor, back, and buttocks are all fully engaged to extend and stabilize the torso. Your limbs and extremities, however, should remain relaxed. Your hands, feet, and calves should be extended, but free from tension. At each repetition of the exercise, you will need to use your growing body awareness skills to check that your toes and fingers are still "soft" and relaxed. This is important because inappropriate contraction of the muscles in the limbs will act in opposition to the work of the muscles of the torso.

A "lengthened" body

Many exercises in the Pilates system are intended to lengthen the spine. Such exercises activate the muscles of the torso that support the spine, mobilizing and decompressing stiff joints. The result is freer movement and a more upright posture that gives the impression of increased height.

PRACTISING THE JAVELIN

Start this exercise in the prone position. Take the time to adjust your alignment as described on page 104. It is important to do this at the start because the exercise will reinforce any errors in your alignment if you don't. Then perform a few repetitions of the prone inner thigh squeeze (page 114) and the back extension (page 106). This will help you to identify and isolate the key muscles you will be using for this exercise. You are not ready for the javelin if you are still having difficulty with either of the preparation exercises and should spend some time ensuring you are happy with them before moving on to the next level.

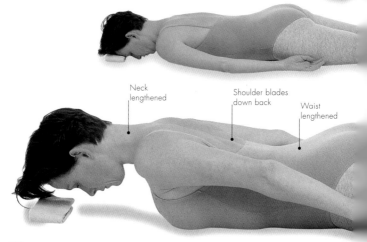

Neck lengthened

Shoulder blades down back

Waist lengthened

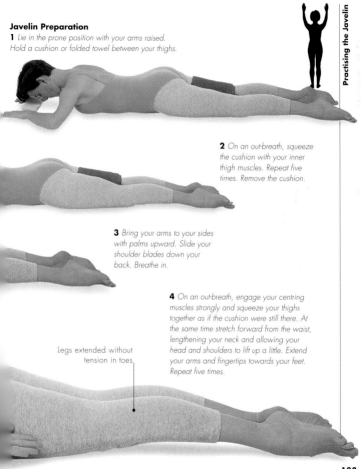

Javelin Preparation

1 *Lie in the prone position with your arms raised.*
Hold a cushion or folded towel between your thighs.

2 *On an out-breath, squeeze
the cushion with your inner
thigh muscles. Repeat five
times. Remove the cushion.*

3 *Bring your arms to your sides
with palms upward. Slide your
shoulder blades down your
back. Breathe in.*

4 *On an out-breath, engage your centring
muscles strongly and squeeze your thighs
together as if the cushion were still there. At
the same time stretch forward from the waist,
lengthening your neck and allowing your
head and shoulders to lift up a little. Extend
your arms and fingertips towards your feet.
Repeat five times.*

Legs extended without
tension in toes

183

Working the Arms while Standing

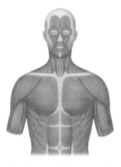

Shoulder and chest muscles

Arm exercises involve all the muscles of the shoulders, chest, and upper arms.

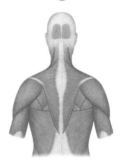

Muscles of the upper back

The trapezius muscle works with the shoulder muscles and latissimus dorsi to stabilize the shoulder blades.

Arm exercises look easy and relaxing, but the reality is that you need to have achieved a good level of stability of the torso before you can undertake them effectively.

The origins of arm movement

Movement of the upper arm originates in the shoulder joint. This is a highly mobile ball-and-socket joint that, when functioning freely, allows the arm to rotate through 360 degrees. Nowadays, we hardly ever use the shoulder joint to its full potential. All too often we create arm motion by moving the upper body instead of the shoulder joint. This leads to stiffening of the shoulder joint through lack of use, which in turn creates a vicious circle of inappropriate movements that unbalance the body and fail to utilize the full range of its muscles.

Recreating full mobility

Movement of the arm should be initiated and controlled through the muscles of the upper arm, shoulder, and chest. These become active during arm movements when the shoulder blades are stabilized. The exercises on pages 186–187 are designed to help you drop your shoulder blades and stabilize them in this position. Then you will learn to free the shoulder joint and use this new-found mobility to rotate the arm using the correct muscles. This creates active, toned muscles around the shoulders, chest, and upper arms. These exercises also help to counter unwanted tension in the upper trapezius muscle.

Posture Reminder

Arm exercises provide a valuable opportunity to recheck and improve your standing posture. They must be carried out from a stable and aligned position, in which the centring muscles are supporting the back and abdomen. Before you start this part of your programme, stand in front of a mirror and carefully recheck your standing posture according to the guidelines on pages 124–125.

ARM RAISES AND ROTATIONS

Perform the exercises on this page while focusing on immobilizing your torso and dropping your shoulders. It is best to work in front of a mirror so that you can constantly check for signs of hunching of the shoulders, which is the most common fault that can occur. Eventually, however, your body awareness will increase to the point where you can tell immediately if your shoulders are raised because it will feel wrong. Between each exercise in this series, drop your arms down to your sides and shake out your shoulders to release any tension. Then carefully re-establish your starting position.

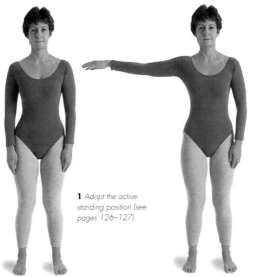

2 As you breathe out engage your centring muscles and lengthen one arm up to shoulder height with hand and fingers level with the arm. Keep your shoulders down. Bring the arm down on the in-breath and repeat using the other arm. Do six repetitions on both sides.

1 Adopt the active standing position (see pages 126–127).

3 Using the same technique as in Step 2, extend both arms simultaneously. Complete six repetitions, bringing your arms to your sides between each one.

4 On an out-breath, extend both arms out to the sides with flexed wrists. Take an in-breath, then on the out-breath, make three small circles with your arms without locking the elbows. Take an in-breath and then on the out-breath make three small circles in the opposite direction.

5 On an out-breath, extend both arms out to the sides and at the same time come up onto your toes. Use your centring muscles to keep your torso stable. On the in-breath, lower your arms and return to active standing. Repeat six times.

Balance and Strength

Centre of gravity
For the Spring you need to adopt a semi-crouching position in which your weight is distributed evenly around a vertical line through your ankles, hips, and shoulders.

Whether or not it was one of your primary goals when commencing your Pilates programme, one of the benefits of Pilates exercise that you will undoubtedly be noticing is the improvement in your overall balance and physical co-ordination. You will find that you are using your body more economically and with greater sensitivity. In the next series of exercises, based on the Spring, you will be developing your appreciation of your centre of gravity and how to use this understanding to provide added stability in your everyday activities.

Stillness in movement

The Spring has its origins in both the yoga tradition and the work of Frederick Alexander. In this position the body's weight is distributed evenly over the hips, knees, and ankles, while the body leans forward and the knees are bent. The position resembles the midway point in the movement between sitting and standing.

The maintenance of this posture requires flexibility of the hips and strength in the torso and legs, as well as a sensitivity to shifts in your centre of gravity. Firm engagement of the centring muscles is required to maintain the alignment of the spine, but the tops of the shoulders should be relaxed downwards at all times to give an overall sense of ease and energy. The posture is still but many muscles are actively engaged in readiness to "spring" forward when in this position.

The Spring

One of the benefits of practising this position is that you can begin to use it in your everyday activities. It has already been noted that the Spring is a transition point between sitting and standing. You will be moving in a healthier way if you consciously aim for this position each time you sit down or get up from sitting. Engage your centring muscles, lead with your head, and actively use your leg muscles to control the overall movement. Activities such as lifting and bending will also become less stressful as a result of your familiarity with this exercise.

Once you have established how to maintain the Spring position without strain, you can also use the further exercises on pages 190–191 to tone the muscles in the backs of the arms and between the shoulder blades.

THE SPRING

You may need to prepare yourself for the Spring by practising a preparatory exercise that uses a wall for support. This will help you achieve the correct angle in which to balance your weight over your legs. Once you have a sense of how the position should feel, try it without the wall to support you and then move on to the triceps squeeze and shoulder rotations.

1 Stand with your feet hip-width apart, about 15 centimetres (6 inches) away from a wall. Bend your knees slightly and rest your back against the wall.

2 Now start to hinge forward from the hips, keeping your back flat and your neck long. Allow your arms to follow the movement.

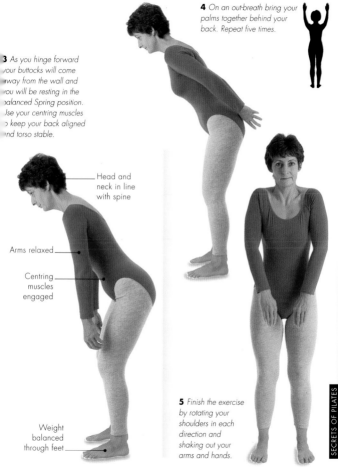

4 On an out-breath bring your palms together behind your back. Repeat five times.

3 As you hinge forward your buttocks will come away from the wall and you will be resting in the balanced Spring position. Use your centring muscles to keep your back aligned and torso stable.

Head and neck in line with spine

Arms relaxed

Centring muscles engaged

Weight balanced through feet

5 Finish the exercise by rotating your shoulders in each direction and shaking out your arms and hands.

Sitting Without Stress

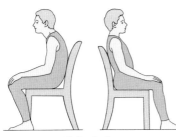

Sitting faults
*The two sitting positions shown here –
slumped and over-arched – are equally
stressful for the spine.*

Most of us spend a great deal of the day sitting down at a desk or in front of a computer workstation, so it is vitally important to adopt a correct sitting posture. Sitting is one of the most stressful positions for the spine. This stress can be reduced if attention is paid to spinal alignment.

From sitting to stretching

The stretching exercises discussed on the following pages are all carried out in a seated position. They are therefore ideal for releasing back tension while you are at work, and can be performed at regular intervals throughout the day. But before you can start on these, you will need to check and adjust the way that you normally sit. The objective is to ensure that the weight of the head is evenly transmitted down the spine and through the pelvis. If you slump so that your back is rounded or, alternatively, over-straighten so that the lumbar curve is excessive, the weight will create stress in parts of the spine. In the long term, back trouble is the likely consequence of sitting in such positions. By supporting your spine in the neutral position, with the muscles of the torso actively engaged, you can minimize the potential for strain or for compression of the discs that provide cushioning between the vertebrae.

A balanced sitting posture

The following is a checklist in order to ensure you are sitting correctly.
• Choose an upright chair that has a firm seat.

Your feet should be able to rest
comfortably flat on the floor with your
knees at right angles.

Sit down with your buttocks near
the edge of the chair – your knees
should be hip-width apart and your
ankles should be placed directly
under your knees.

Feel the weight resting on your sitting
bones and through the balance points
under your feet (see pages 136–137).

Lengthen up through the spine while,
at the same time, drawing your shoulder
blades downwards.

Engage the centring muscles to create
an overall sense of lightness within
your body.

Adopt this position as far as possible
for all of your seated activities. Avoid
sitting in soft, low chairs for long
periods. They may seem restful at the
time but gradually they can do a great
deal of harm to your back. Also ensure
that your office chair is properly
adjusted for your height, otherwise your
back will be placed under extra stress
and this will cause it to be strained.

SEATED SIDE STRETCHES

The side stretches shown here engage the deep muscles in the sides of the body, and so contribute to the overall strength of the torso while also encouraging greater mobility. One of the key factors to effective side stretches is to use your centring muscles to maintain a sense of lifting and lengthening as well as bending or rotating. This keeps the spine well supported through the movement and prevents compression of the intervertebral discs. The other vital element is the maintenance of a stable pelvis to provide a firm anchor for the stretches. Working in the sitting position helps to immobilize the pelvis, but you will also have to use the lower abdominal muscles.

Side stretch

1 *Sit towards the edge of a firm chair with knees hip-width apart. Slide your shoulder blades down your back, engage your centring muscles and lengthen up through the spine. Place your hands behind your head.*

2 *On an out-breath stretch over to one side. Control the movement with your centring muscles. Come back to the centre on an in-breath. Repeat to the other side. Complete six repetitions.*

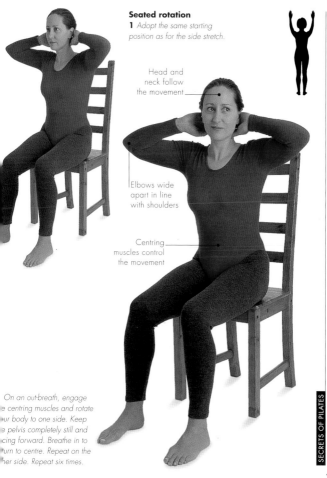

Seated rotation

1 Adopt the same starting position as for the side stretch.

Head and neck follow the movement

Elbows wide apart in line with shoulders

Centring muscles control the movement

On an out-breath, engage the centring muscles and rotate your body to one side. Keep the pelvis completely still and facing forward. Breathe in to return to centre. Repeat on the other side. Repeat six times.

Working the Sides of the Legs

Cushion support
Use a cushion to support your upper leg to ensure alignment of the pelvis in the inner thigh lift.

There are not many everyday activities that effectively strengthen and tone the inner and outer muscles of the thigh and hip. However these are important muscles for the maintenance of proper alignment of the legs and pelvis. They also contribute to the effectiveness of the leg movements.

The success of the exercises in this group depend on the precise alignment of the spine in the side position. When you first start learning these exercises it is useful to align your sacrum and back against a wall so that you can be sure that you have adopted the right position. Having established this position, you need to keep your centring muscles strongly engaged throughout the sequence in order to maintain it. The need for such control is the reason why these exercises are classed as progression exercises, as you need to have developed a good level of stability in the torso before you can perform them successfully.

From waist to thigh

The outer thigh exercises that form the first part of this set not only work the muscles along the outside of the thigh from hip to knee, but also strengthen and tone the waist, buttocks (gluteals), and the deep muscles that control the hip joint. When you are performing the exercises you will soon become aware of the muscles being worked. Howeve don't allow the effort to create tension your body. Keep the following body-awareness pointers in mind:

• Maintain a sense of lengthening from your neck all the way through to the heel of the working leg.

• Visualize the movement originating in the waist and keep your waist "long" so that your pelvis remains stable as you move your leg.

Working the inner thigh

The adductor muscles of the inner thigh are the focus of the next exercise you will be shown. But it is important to remember to support the entire action by using your centring muscles, as this will ensure that the effort remains located in the intended area. Keep in mind that, although you are lying down, you are not supposed to be resting. Some beginners find it difficult to maintain a stable position while performing this exercise as there is often a tendency for the hip to tip forwards. It can therefore be helpful to use a firm pillow or folded towel to support the upper leg while doing this exercise.

SIDE LEG LIFTS

Before you begin these exercises you should spend some time checking your alignment in the side position. As a newcomer to this part of the programme, it is best to lie against a wall to help you establish the correct position. When you have become accustomed to the exercise, you will probably find that you can adopt the position without the help of the wall. Make sure you are comfortable lying on your side and use a layer of padding under your hip if you need the extra support. Complete six repetitions of each exercise on one side and then turn and repeat on the other.

Starting position

Lie on your side with your underneath arm stretched out above your head and place your other hand in front of your body to prevent yourself from tipping forwards. Bend your knees at right angles and then check that your top foot is directly above the lower one and that your knees, hips, and shoulders are similarly stacked. You can use a mat for extra support.

Mat for extra support

Outer thigh lifts

Straighten your top leg so that the foot is a short distance from the floor. Flex your foot and angle it downwards. Breathe in.

2 On the out-breath, raise your top leg a little further. Keep your body stable. Breathe in and lower your leg.

Inner thigh lifts

1 Extend the lower leg and bend the upper leg at right angles. Support the upper knee with a plump cushion to prevent the hips from rolling forwards.

2 Breathe in. On the out-breath engage the centring muscles and lift the lower leg a few centimetres (couple of inches). Lower on the out-breath, maintaining the stability of the torso and pelvis as you do so.

Releasing Tension in the Chest

Supporting the neck and head

For the chest opening exercise it is important to keep the head and neck in alignment with the spine. A firm cushion under the head will help you achieve this.

When under threat our natural instinct is to close in around the chest and abdomen. This is to protect the vital organs from injury in case of attack. We carry this instinctive reaction into our daily life – even in a modern urban society. As we deal with the stress and worry that is part of a normal busy routine, muscle tension and a sense of restriction in the chest can build up insidiously as we sit hunched over a desk or cramped in a car, for example, for hours on end. Breathing becomes shallow and the muscles in the shoulders and chest tighten. Ineffective breathing only adds to the physical tension and increases tiredness and irritability. Often we are unaware of this happening. It is only when we consciously work to release these tensions through gentle stretches such as the chest opening exercise on the following pages that we realize the damaging effect of this physical manifestation of stress.

Releasing muscle tension

The chest opening exercise also helps to relax hard-worked muscles after a serious exercise session, helping you to avoid possible stiffness and feel both reinvigorated and at peace.

Approach this exercise in a leisurely fashion, and allow yourself to relish the sense of release that it will bring. Focus

on the sensation of "openness" that the movement induces. Try to visualize the muscles of the upper chest slowly stretching out, encouraged by your steady breathing and relaxation of the shoulders.

Progressing gradually

As with all Pilates exercise, it is your approach to the movement that is important, not the final position you achieve. In this case you should focus on getting your starting position correct and maintaining the alignment of the pelvis and knees. Although you are aiming to reach the floor with your top arm as you lift it to the other side of your body, if you are stiff you may not manage this at first. However, you will still be gaining the full benefit of a valuable stretch, providing you perform the exercise precisely. In a few weeks you will find that increasing mobility in your spine and shoulders will permit you to stretch further.

CHEST OPENING

For this exercise you need to position yourself carefully before you start so that your head, neck, and spine are in alignment. Your knees should be bent so as to create a right angle between your torso and thighs and between the thighs and lower legs. Your arms should also be stretched out in front at right angles to the body. Throughout the movement your aim should be to keep your pelvis and legs completely stable. All movement should be focused in your upper body.

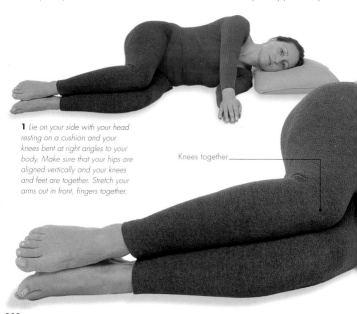

1 Lie on your side with your head resting on a cushion and your knees bent at right angles to your body. Make sure that your hips are aligned vertically and your knees and feet are together. Stretch your arms out in front, fingers together.

Knees together

Elbows soft

2 Breathe in and engage your centring muscles to stabilize your pelvis. Lift your top arm slowly in an arc over your body. Follow its movement with your head. Keep your gaze on your hand. Keep your arm relaxed and your elbow soft.

3 Take your arm as far towards the floor as is comfortable. You will know you have reached your limit if you feel your hips or knees shifting out of alignment. Return to the starting position on an out-breath. Repeat five times.

Pelvis stable

Head and eyes follow movement

Finishing Stretch

Record-keeping
Keep a note of difficulties you have experienced and overcome and of the benefits you notice from your training.

As you finish each of your Pilates sessions you need to wind down without losing the sense of energy that you have generated during your workout. You therefore need to provide your body with a sense of balance and harmony that integrates the beneficial effects on different parts of the body of the various exercises you have performed. Moreover, the final exercise that you perform will have a bearing on the feelings that you take away from your workout. A complex exercise, which you may have some difficulty mastering, could leave you with a sense of dissatisfaction or even failure. So it is important to choose an accessible exercise that leaves you in a state of physical harmony and with positive emotions. You should also be aiming to relax your whole body before you finish, which is an important part of the last exercise.

The final stretch

The full body stretch on the following pages provides an ideal close to your exercise session as it allows active relaxation for the whole body – from head to toe. You will by now have a full appreciation of the degree of active engagement that you need to incorporate into any stretching exercise, and this one is no different. But this effort is always balanced by a wonderful sense of release and relaxation when the stretch is complete. For variety you may sometimes choose to end your Pilates session with a different closing exercise. The chest opening stretch on page 202 and the

roll down on page 130 are excellent
alternatives. Be sure to perform
whichever exercise you choose slowly
and with care.

When you have repeated your final
stretch a few times, you should allow
yourself time for relaxation as you
gradually ready your mind and body
for a return to your regular activities.

Self-assessment

Once an exercise session has finished,
it is easy to forget the detail of what
exercises you performed, how many
repetitions, how easy or difficult you
found them, and whether you had any
particular problems. Try keeping a diary
of your progress that you can update
after each session. This information will
be useful in planning your ongoing
Pilates programme, as it will help you to
pinpoint which exercises you need to
work on and which aspects are causing
you problems. If you are working under
the guidance of a Pilates teacher, these
notes can provide valuable feedback
for discussion at your next lesson.

FULL BODY STRETCH

Use this exercise as your final wind-down after your Pilates session. It can also be used as an instant relaxer and re-energizer anytime you need to release physical and mental tension: for example, after returning home from work or after any other tiring activity. Remember that the more energy you put into the stretch, the greater the sense of relaxation there will be when you release it. Be sure to check your alignment in the supine position before you start (see pages 48–49). When you have finished, you should be careful how you get up as sudden movements will disrupt the feeling of tranquillity you have acquired and may also make you feel dizzy.

Lie on your back in the alignment position (see pages 50–51). Extend your arms over your head. On an out-breath, stretch out from toes to finger tips. Keep your shoulders relaxed and away from your ears. Repeat up to five times and then relax (see box).

Hands and
fingers extended

Shoulders down

Wais
lengthened

Relaxation

After the full body stretch, allow yourself a few minutes' relaxation before getting up. Choose a comfortable lying-down position on your back or side. If necessary, use cushions to support yourself in a strain-free position. Focus on your breathing and the sensation of your weight sinking into the floor.

Knees extended, but soft

Feet pointed, toes relaxed

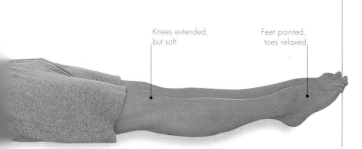

Working With Weights

Choosing weights
You can buy weights from a sports supplier or improvise with household items such as bags of rice or sugar.

Using weights, whether they are hand-held or strapped to the wrists or ankles, will increase the workload of any exercise. The muscles have to work harder to overcome the resistance created by the weight and therefore will eventually become stronger than they would have been if no weights had been used. There is also a general relationship between the lifting of heavy weights and the development of muscle bulk. However, that isn't the aim of using weights in Pilates exercise, in which the relatively light weights used and the careful balance of the exercises means that the added muscle bulk is minimal.

Strong muscles, strong bones

Over the past few decades, medical research into the causes of the common bone-thinning condition osteoporosis has indicated a strong correlation between the amount of weight-bearing exercise taken during adult life and bone density. It is clear that those who regularly take such exercise have a much lower risk of osteoporosis than those who don't. This is especially important for women, who are far more susceptible to loss of bone mass after the menopause than men of a similar age. All Pilates exercise is helpful for maintaining bone density, but adding weights increases this benefit.

When to add weights

Do not feel pressured to add weights to your practice. You can exercise effectively against the resistance of your own body weight and with regular practice you will continue to progress. But if you do want to add weights you need to observe some guidelines. There is no point in adding weights until

you have mastered the basic technique
for any exercise and have built up the
necessary level of strength. Be sure that
you can perform the recommended
number of repetitions of the exercise,
while maintaining complete muscular
control (with stable, neutral pelvis, ribs
drawn in, shoulder blades down the
back, and all centring muscles
engaged) before attempting to make
this transition. If you are working with a
Pilates teacher, ask their advice on the
right time for you to start using weights.

What weights to use

Always start with the lightest weights.
For your first practices with hand-held
weights, experiment with cans of food
or packets of rice or sugar, for example,
weighing 250–500 grams (8–17
ounces). If you make progress with
these starter weights, you may wish to
graduate to something a little heavier. If
you want to buy weights, choose dumb-
bells and/or strap-on ankle weights of
no more than 1 kilogram (2 pounds) for
the first few months of weight practice.

ADDING WEIGHTS

Holding a weight in each hand increases the workload of all exercises involving arm movements. Depending on the exercise, this can further strengthen and tone the arm, shoulder, chest, and back muscles. Adding weights to your ankles increases the workload in exercises that involve leg movements. This can provide an extra challenge to the leg, hip, buttock, and lower abdominal muscles.

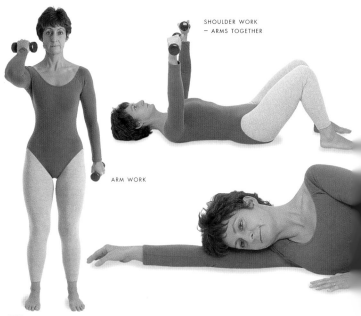

SHOULDER WORK
– ARMS TOGETHER

ARM WORK

SHOULDER WORK –
ALTERNATING ARMS

OUTER LEG WORK

INNER LEG WORK

Achieving Integration

The whole body
*Your aim is to develop a sense of all
parts of your body functioning together
as an integrated whole.*

This is a book for newcomers to
Pilates. Even when you've read all
the material it contains, assimilated
the information and instructions, and
tried all the exercises, you will still be a
relative novice. Re-educating your body
away from its previous bad habits and
continually reinforcing the healthier
ways of moving is a lifetime project.
The learning curve is steep when you

first start and flattens as you build on the
increasingly familiar principles of
Pilates. But as you progress you will
begin to appreciate that there are new
levels to which you can take your
understanding and physical abilities.

What is integration?

When the word "integration" is used in
a Pilates context, it generally refers to
the balanced development of all the
muscles in the body. The strengthening
of one group of muscles should never
be allowed to distort the functioning of
a less developed muscle group. This
integration can be achieved only
through years of balanced practice.
You need determination and dedication
to commit yourself to a programme of
exercises that includes many movements
you find difficult and exhausting as well
as those you find easy and enjoyable.

Continuous movement

The idea of integration can also be
applied to the way you practise your
Pilates exercises. As a novice, you will

have been focusing all your attention on executing the individual exercises to the best of your ability. And this is the way it should be.

However, once you are thoroughly familiar with a basic selection of exercises and can perform them all fluently, you may wish to consider integrating them into a single continuous movement, in which one exercise flows into the next like a dance. This kind of practice enables you to develop further the essential Pilates principles of fluidity and co-ordination and bring into your exercise programme an element of creativity as you devise your own combinations of movements.

When you work in this way, your exercise routine will be far removed from the tedious drudgery that some people imagine it to be. You will find that it is in fact a time for self-expression and physical harmony and will look forward to your exercise session each day. See the sequence on pages 214–215 as an example of how to advance from your basic exercises.

PILATES AS DANCE

The series of exercises on this page gives an example of how you can link individual exercises to form a continuous dance-like movement. Use your imagination to devise your own "dances" from combinations of exercises that you are confident in performing well. Take care to ensure that transitions between exercises are performed smoothly and without jerkiness. Remember that control and precision in your movements remain your governing principles.

1

2

3

4

5

6

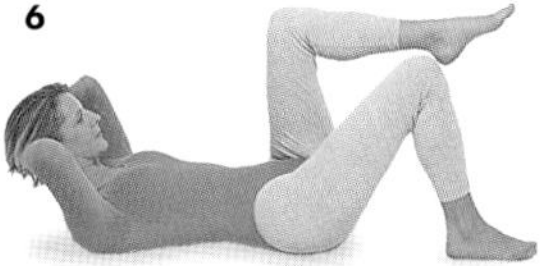

7

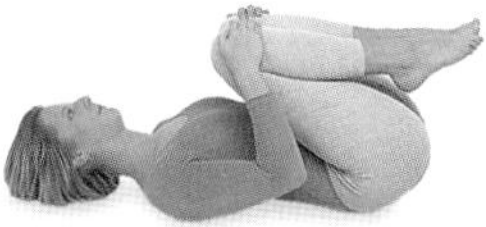

8

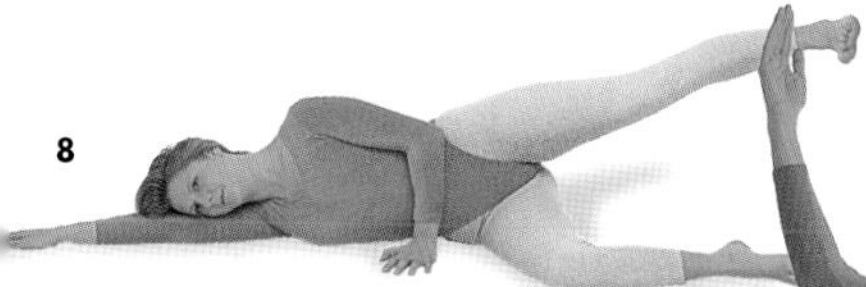

12

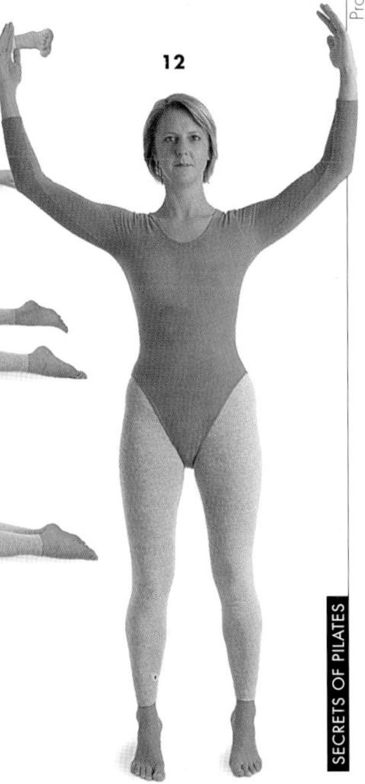

9

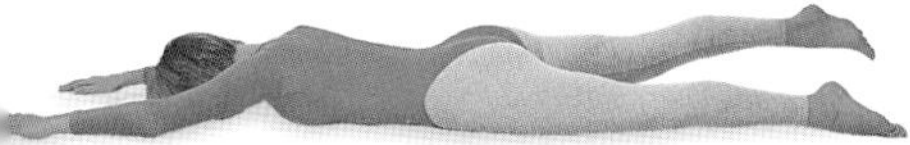

10

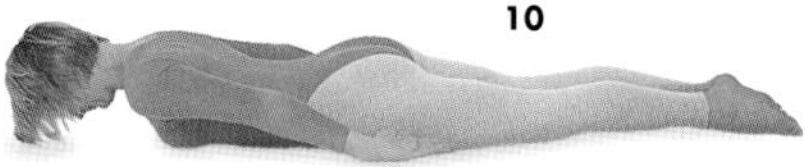

11

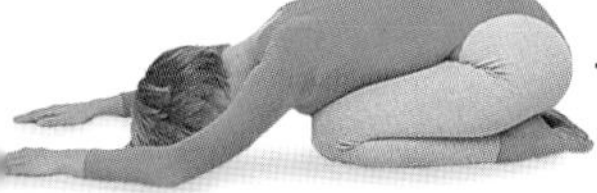

Glossary

Abdominals The muscles that surround and support the area from the ribcage to the pubic bone. They control the movement of the torso and are the basis of the girdle of strength.

Body awareness Refers to sensitivity to the effects on your body of different physical actions. This includes awareness of your posture and alignment and which muscles are being utilized in each movement.

Centring muscles Used to describe the muscles that support the centre of the body. These include the abdominal muscles, pelvic floor, latissimus dorsi and gluteals.

Contrology The name Joseph Pilates gave to his system of body-conditioning exercises.

Engagement A muscle is said to be engaged when it is active and contracted during a movement. In Pilates-based exercise you learn to engage muscles

without bringing tension or stiffness into the action.

Girdle of strength Describes the muscles that support the centre of the body.

Gluteals, gluteus maximus The large muscles of the buttocks, attached to the sacrum and the upper part of the femur.

Hamstrings The muscles at the back of the thigh that contract to bend the knee.

Hip width The distance between an individual's hip joints, often used as a measure for the placement of the feet in Pilates exercise because it ensures correct parallel alignment of the hips, knees, and ankles.

Latissimus dorsi The muscles that extend from the shoulder blades to the top of the pelvis. Commonly known as the lats, they stabilize the shoulder blades and provide postural support.

Lumbar curve The natural concave curve in the spine at the waist.

Mobilization The restoration or enhancement of the range of movement in a joint. Pilates aims to mobilize joints such as the hips, shoulders, and intervertebral joints to give stress-free movement.

Navel to spine The action of drawing in the abdominal muscles on exhalation, which promotes hollowing or "scooping" of the tummy. This action engages the deep muscles within the abdomen that support the spine and ensures that all the centring muscles are working together correctly to produce a strong and streamlined torso.

Neutral pelvis, neutral spine The position of the pelvis that creates the correct curves in the spine. If the top of the pelvis tips forward, the lumbar curve is exaggerated. If it tips back, the lumbar curve is flattened. In most Pilates exercises, the pelvis and spine need to be held in the neutral position.

Obliques The muscles that stretch diagonally around the sides of the body and meet in the front of the abdomen. These are important centring muscles that govern the twisting movements of the torso.

Pelvic floor The hammock of muscles that run from the pubic bone to the sacrum. These provide vital support for the pelvic organs and also contribute to posture and alignment.

Pelvis The bony basin that protects the vital lower abdominal organs. It is attached to the lower part of the spine and is the anchoring point for the hip joints.

Powerhouse A term used by Joseph Pilates for the girdle of strength.

Prone Describes the position in which you are lying, face downward, on the abdomen.

Quadriceps The large muscles at the front of the thigh, also known as the quads, that contract to lift the thigh and extend the knee joint.

Rectus abdominus The vertical sheet of muscle at the front of the abdomen. Contraction of this centring muscle flexes the body forward.

Sacrum The large flat bone near the base of the spine that is joined to the back of the pelvis.

Scoop A term used by some Pilates teachers to describe the hollowing effect of drawing the navel to the spine.

Supine Lying face up on your back.

Thoracic breathing Also known as rib breathing, this method of expanding the ribcage

out to the sides to draw in air, rather than expanding the abdomen, is used in most Pilates exercises. In this method the ribcage contracts on the out-breath, allowing effective engagement of the centring muscles during any movement requiring effort.

Transversus abdominus The transversus muscles of the abdomen wrap around the centre of the body and provide support for the abdominal organs.

Trapezius The diamond-shaped muscle that extends from the neck outwards to each shoulder and down between the shoulder blades. This muscle tends to contract and remain bunched and tense when we are under stress. This distorts the position of the shoulders and in turn can lead to headaches and a variety of postural problems.

FURTHER READING

L ROBINSON and G THOMSON, *Body Control the Pilates Way*, Pan Books, 1998

L ROBINSON and G THOMSON, *The Official Body Control Pilates Manual*, Macmillan, 2000

B SILER, *The Pilates Body*, Michael Joseph, 2000

A SELBY and A HERDMAN, *Pilates: Creating the Body You Want*, Gaia Books, 1999

J. H. PILATES and WILLIAM JOHN MILLER, *Pilates' Return to Life Through Contrology*, Presentation Dynamics Inc., 1998

JOSEPH H. PILATES, *Your Health*, Presentation Dynamics Inc., 1998

USEFUL ADDRESSES

The Balanced Body Studio Equilibrium
150 Chiswick High Road
London W4 1PR
England
www.pilates.uk.com

The Body Control Pilates Association
14 Neal's Yard
London WC2H 9DP
England
Tel: +44 (0) 207 379 3734
Fax: +44 (0) 207 379 7751
www.bodycontrol.co.uk

The Body Maintenance Pilates Studio
2nd Floor Pineapple Studios
7 Langley Street
London WC2H 9JA
England
Tel: +44 (0) 207 379 6043

Alan Herdman Studios
17 Homer Row
London W1H 1HU
England
Tel: +44 (0) 207 723 9953

Pilates Foundation UK Ltd
30 Camden Road
London E17 7NF, England
Tel/Fax: +44 (0) 207 178 1859

Oxford School Of Pilates
c/o Melbourne House
58 Acre End Street
Eynsham OX8 1PD
England
Tel: +44 (0) 1865 882 927

Edinburgh Pilates Centre
45a George Street
Edinburgh EH2 2HT
Scotland
Tel: +44 (0) 131 226 1815

The Pilates Studio
890 Broadway, 6th Floor
New York, NY 10003
USA
Tel: +1 (212) 358 7676
Fax: +1 (212) 358 7678
www.pilates-studio.com

The Australian Pilates Method Association
PO Box 27
Mosman NSW 2088
Australia
Fax: +61 (0)2 9929 8807
www.auspil.asn.au/

INDEX

a

abdomen 21, 24, 26–27
  breathing 60
  curls 166–167
  development 164–167
  doming 61
  muscles 64, 88–89
  obliques 172
  pelvic floor 53
  strengthening 100–103
  weak 84
additional exercises 69
alcohol 36
Alexander, Frederick 32, 188
Alexander Technique 32, 145
alignment 8, 38
  key 48–51
  neck 72
  pelvis 21
anatomy 20–23
ancient Greeks 16
ankles 41
  groundwork 132–135
  pedalling 138
arms 184–187
Arrow 180

b

back 128–131, 146
  curves 20, 39–40
  extension 106–107
  lower 84–87
  pain 28, 72
balance 136–139, 188–191
benefits 28–31
body 6, 20–3, 57
  awareness 16, 104–105, 140, 181, 196–197
  characteristics 38–39
  checks 40–43
  control 137
  full stretch 204–207
  key structures 20–21
  tone 14
body see also mind–body link
bone density 208
bouncing 97, 117
breast bone 20
breathing 17, 19, 56–57
  assessment 140
  awareness 105
  control 169
  progression 144–147
  sequences 60—63
  shoulders 76

c

capabilities 9
centring 10, 17, 19, 26–27
centring muscles 24, 26
  assessment 140
  breathing 60
  Hundred 168
  pelvic floor 52–53
  sitting 156–157
chest 200–203

childbirth 36, 52
classes 9
clavicle 20
clothes 44–45
co-ordination 16–17, 19
collar bone 20
concentration 16
  hips 93
  mental focus 57
  neck 72
  principles 18
confidence 9
control 16, 18
  dance 214
  Hundred 169
  mind 56
  muscles 16
Contrology 12, 56

d

dance 12, 214–215
depression 8
diagonal shoulder raise 172–175
diagonal stretch 176–179
diet 29
discomfort 141
doctors 32, 36
drugs 36
Dynaband 45, 98–99

e

equipment 44–45

f

feet 38, 41, 43, 126

balance 136–139, 149
  groundwork 132–135
Feldenkrais Method 32
Feldenkrais, Moshe 32
fevers 37
finishing stretch 204–207
flexibility 17, 18
fluidity 17, 18
foundation exercises 6
  introduction 70
  preparation 46
  programme planner 66–69
four-square breathing 144–147
full body stretch 204–207

g

girdle of strength 24–25, 53, 81, 112
glossary 216–217
gluteals 108, 112, 196
groundwork 132–135

h

habits 25, 112
hamstrings 96–99, 156–159
hand-held weights 208–211
head 40, 43, 74–75
headaches 72
health 8

heel lifts 126
hip rolls 90–91
hips 92–93, 108–109
  inner thighs 112
  joints 21
  pelvic stability 152–153
  rotation 160–163
humerus 20
Hundred 168–171

i

injury 31, 32, 36, 37
inner thighs 80–83, 112–115, 197
integration 212–213
invertebral discs 20, 73

j

Javelin 180–183
joint problems 28–29

k

key body structures 20–23
kneeling rest position 64, 65
knees 38–39, 41
  hamstrings 96–99
  raise 162–163
  roll 152–155

l

legs 41, 92–95, 108–111, 196–199
lengthening 21, 25, 58,

64, 86, 93, 164, 177, 178–179, 180–181, 194, 197
lifestyle 33
ligaments 20, 52
lumbar curve 20, 49, 96, 146

m

mantra 24
medication 37
meditation 57–59
mental engagement 56–59
mind–body link 8–9, 32–33
  control 56
  re-education 46
mind–body link see also body
mobility 185
muscles 16–17, 22–23
  abdomen 100–101
  arms 184
  assessment 140
  breathing 60
  centring 24, 26, 52, 61, 92, 100, 140
  chest 200–201
  control 16
  forgotten 161
  Hundred 168
  integration 212
  main 22–23
  neck 72
  pelvic floor 52–53

sitting 156–157
tone 25, 29
unused 37
weights 208–211

n

navel 59
neck 39, 40, 72–75
neutral pelvis 49–51
    assessment 140
    back 84–85
    hips 160
    pelvic floor 53
    relaxation 65

o

obliques 172–175
occupational problems 28,
    72

p

pain 141
pedalling 138–139
pelvic floor 24, 52–55
    breathing 60
    inner thighs 80–81, 112
    muscles 52–55
pelvis 21, 38, 41
    assessment 140
    back 84–85
    balance 137–138
    freeing 96–99
    hips 160
    isolating 92–95
    legs 108
    neutral 49–51, 53

posture 42–43
relaxation 65
stability 152–155
tilts 127
visualization 58
personal programme 9,
    68–69
physique 14–15
Pilates, Joseph 6
    control 56
    exercise system 8
    powerhouse 24
    principles 16–19
    work 12–13
Pilates Studio 12–13
postnatal 31, 52
posture 38–43, 48
    arms 185
    basic position 124–
    127
    habits 20
    mind 56
powerhouse 24
precautions 34, 36
precision 8, 16–17, 19,
    214
pregnancy 36
preparation 6, 34
principles 16–19
programme planner 66–69
progress 9
progressed abdominal curls
    166–167
progression exercises 6,
    142
prone position 104–105

diagonal stretch
    176–179
inner thigh squeeze
    114–115
Javelin 180–183
leg stretch 110–111
resting 122–123

q

quadriceps 116–119

r

relaxation 64–65, 113,
    120–121, 207
repetitive strain 28
rest position 122–123
rib breathing 60, 62–63,
    121
roll down 128–131

s

scapula 20
seated hamstring stretches
    158–159
self belief 56–57
self-assessment 140–141,
    205
shoulder blade 20
shoulders 20–21, 39–40
    characteristics 39–40
    diagonal raise 172–175
    neck 72
    posture 42–43
    releasing 76–79
side leg lifts 196–199
sides 192–195

sitting 26
  easy 156–159
  side stretches
    192–195
sleep 65
space 44–45
spine 20, 39, 58
  alignment 72
  awareness 128–131
  curling 59
  enhanced control
    148–151
  gluteals 108
  Hundred 168
  inner thighs 80
  Javelin 181
  lengthening 120–123
  lift 84–87
  muscles 104
  progressed lift
    150–151
  rotation 88–91
  shoulders 76
  stretching 64, 120
sports 13, 173
Spring 188–191
stability 10
standing 27, 38
  arms 184–187
  basic position
    124–127
  faults 42–43
  Spring 188–191
sternum 21
stress 8, 76
stretching 33, 37,
    192–195
supine position 48–49,
  58, 61, 73, 78

t
teachers 9, 36, 37, 48,
  62, 102
thighs 80–83,
  112–119, 197
thoracic breathing 60
toe raises 126
turned-out knee raises
  162–163

u
urination 52, 54

v
vertebrae 20, 72, 104,
  120, 129
visualization 56–59, 65,
  85, 180

w
wall support 129
weight loss 29
weights 208–211
well-being 8

y
yoga 33

ACKNOWLEDGEMENTS

Every effort has been made to trace copyright holders and obtain permission.
The publishers apologise for any omissions and would be pleased
to make any necessary changes at subsequent printings.

PICTURE ACKNOWLEDGEMENTS

The Image Bank, London: 12. **Images Colour Library,**
London: 30T, 173, 197. **The Stock Market,** London: 213.
Stone/Getty One: 31T, 89, 161.